More praise for *In the Province of the Gods*

"Like the best memoirs, it reminds us of the genre's twinned truths: first, that the surest way to discover the self is to look out at the world, and second, that the best way to teach others about something is to tell them not 'what it is,' but what it means to you. Fries's deft, questioning prose is as full of compassion as curiosity, and his revelations about himself are no less compelling than what he learns about Japan."

Dale Peck,
author of *Visions and Revisions: Coming of Age in the Age of AIDS*

"Elegant and probing, *In the Province of the Gods* reads like the log of an early adventurer charting a newly discovered land. History, sexual politics, disability, and wooden fortune sticks are blended into an unexpected, tightly written exploration of Japanese culture. Fries may be the guy on the journey, but we're the ones making the discoveries."

Susan R. Nussbaum,
author of *Good Kings, Bad Kings*

LIVING OUT

Gay and Lesbian Autobiographies

In the Province of the Gods

Kenny Fries

The University of Wisconsin Press

The University of Wisconsin Press
1930 Monroe Street, 3rd Floor
Madison, Wisconsin 53711-2059
uwpress.wisc.edu

3 Henrietta Street, Covent Garden
London WC2E 8LU, United Kingdom
eurospanbookstore.com

Printed in the United States of America

This book may be available in a digital edition.

Library of Congress Cataloging-in-Publication Data

Names: Fries, Kenny, 1960- author.
Title: In the province of the gods / Kenny Fries.
Other titles: Living out.
Description: Madison, Wisconsin: The University of Wisconsin Press, [2017]
| Series: Living out: gay and lesbian autobiographies
Identifiers: LCCN 2017010427 | ISBN 9780299314200 (cloth: alk. paper)
Subjects: LCSH: Fries, Kenny, 1960- —Travel—Japan. | Authors, American—21st Century—Biography. | Gays with disabilities—United States—Biography. | Gay men—United States—Biography.
| Authors with disabilities—United States—Biography.
| People with disabilities—Japan—Social conditions.
Classification: LCC PS3556.R568 Z46 2017 | DDC 818/.5403 [B]—dc23
LC record available at https://lccn.loc.gov/2017010427

All Japanese names are written in the traditional order of family name followed by given name. Transliterations from the Japanese are based on the modified Hepburn system, except for *arigato*, which is a simplified version of Hepburn.

for
Mike
who was there

We are born, so to speak, provisionally, it doesn't matter where; it is only gradually that we compose, within ourselves, our true place of origin, so that we may be born there retrospectively.

Rainer Maria Rilke

. . . every day is a journey, and the journey itself is home.

Bashō

Contents

III. World

In the Province of the Gods

Prologue

In the Province of the Gods

If ever I needed the presence of the gods, now is the time.

I arrive at Izumo Taisha, the second-most-sacred shrine in Japan, in early October. According to legend, the sun goddess Amaterasu built the original shrine. In every other part of Japan, the tenth month of the year is known as *kannazuki*, the month without gods, because every October all eight million Shinto deities visit Izumo Taisha for *kanari matsuri*. The gods are now in residence.

I stand under the graceful wooden *torii* marking the entrance to the shrine's forested grounds, then, with my cane, maneuver down the Seki-no-Baba, an avenue of gnarled pines, leading to the shrine's central compound.

I look up: hanging over the entrance to the Oracle Hall is the giant *shimenawa*, a traditional twist of straw rope. The sculpture of straw is immense: five thick twists clinging, with the assistance of six roped rings, to a large wooden rod the same color as the straw, which itself is attached by four thinner roped rings to a dark-brown wooden beam. Descending from the three largest twists are three cone-shaped bells.

I reach for one of the twists and ring the bell.

Ringing the shrine bell announces a visitor's presence to the resident deity. The gods now know I am here.

Ever since my doctor told me what I did not want to hear, all I can think is: *I don't want to die.*

I pull the rope and ring the bell again—this time louder, the echo reaching toward the *honden*, the inner shrine, directly behind the Oracle Hall.

I follow the sound of bronze reverberating through the air until it dissipates in front of a steep covered wooden staircase leading into the *honden*. The present structure, with its projecting gray wooden rafters shooting out of the roof, is in its twenty-fifth incarnation. Only half as high as its pre-Buddhist original, at twenty-four meters it is still the country's tallest shrine. Entrance into the *honden* is allowed only during special ceremonies. Lafcadio Hearn, one of the first expatriate writers to live in Japan, lived only thirty-three kilometers away in Matsue. He was the first foreigner granted the privilege to enter the *honden*.

I peer through the Eight-Legged East Gate, decorated with un-painted wooden carvings and bouquets of *gohei*, lightning-shaped white paper hung at Shinto shrines to ward off evil spirits, and look into the Holy of Holies Hall, where only the head priest can go.

I reach in my pocket for a particular coin. Two months ago, I found a penny in the hospital room where the man in the bed next to me died. Coins have taken on a larger meaning.

I close my eyes and pray for what I know might be possible: to see the best way through this, to find a way to live with the ever-present knowledge of death as my constant companion.

I bow and clap and throw the coin into the offering box.

I hear the coin rattle to the bottom of the box.

My prayers are urgent. The coin at the bottom of the wooden box could be my soul.

I think how I first came to Japan to study the lives of disabled people in Japan. Ian was supposed to accompany me. But by the time I arrived in Japan, circumstances had changed.

During my first stay in Japan, my research proved fitful, difficult. Instead, single for the first time in eighteen years, I discovered not only things about this foreign culture but also new ways to see my different body and myself.

Now, on my second visit, circumstances have changed yet again; I came very close to not returning at all.

But I'm getting ahead of myself. Before I first arrived in Japan, I had no idea I would be going halfway around the world, alone.

I

Floating

The Japanese reticulation of space insists on inside, outside, man-made nature made a part of nature, a continuing symbiosis. Even now, the ideal is that the opposites are one.

Donald Richie

One

Genkan

I am alone in the house when the phone rings. In no mood to talk to anyone, I let the machine get it.

When the outgoing message is over, I hear an unfamiliar voice: "I'm pleased to tell you that you've been chosen as one of the artists to go to Japan. You'll be getting confirmation in the mail in the next few days. In the meantime, if you have any questions, give me a call."

I replay the message and write down the number. I call Ian, who is packing up his studio. No answer.

Ian helped me write my proposal to go to Japan. Besides the research, I was looking forward to living with him abroad to bring the adventure, the sense of purpose, back into our relationship. The past year, things between us have been difficult. The pain in my left foot and my increasingly diminishing mobility reactivated the depression I first battled over a decade ago when I turned thirty, when the pain in my lower back began to be more than a bother.

But a month ago, with his unemployment benefits from his Internet tech bubble job expiring, Ian told me he was thinking about taking a job working for his father in Virginia.

"Are you leaving me?" I asked.

"Not leaving. A separation."

"A separation? I don't want to be separated."

"We haven't been able to get back on track living together. We're imploding."

"I don't want you to go." I didn't know what else to say. "How am I going to manage on my own without you?"

"You always manage."

Countless therapists and friends have told me the same thing. Still, this is something I do not yet believe.

I sit at the dining room table, where I can clearly see how, soon after we met, Ian had painted the house in a color scheme of my own design, how the comfort and intimacy of the early days of our relationship are matched by the three gradations of gold milk-paint used in the living room, dining room, and kitchen. The brave choice of billiard-table green for the bedroom is evidence of the boldness of the foundation of our meeting, as well as the confidence I felt being together.

But later today he will be leaving.

Almost two hours after the phone call, Ian returns from his studio to say good-bye. He enters the house carrying a heavy bag.

"You're not going to believe this," I say across the living room. "I got the grant to go to Japan."

Ian drops the bag. "You've got to be kidding."

"Go listen to the message."

Ian walks into what until that morning was our bedroom and plays the message.

"Congratulations." He comes back into the dining room and looks straight at me. "I got to go."

If only the phone had rung two months, or perhaps even one month, earlier, things might have turned out differently.

"I know you do," I say, getting up to hug the man who I still think of as my true soul mate, the love of my life.

Separation is what we call it because neither of us can bear to say this is permanent: an end.

I am single for the first time in eighteen years.

Back at the dining room table, hearing Ian's old red car start and drive down the street, my first thought is, *how will I manage in Japan?*

When I land at Narita Airport, the sky is a dull gray, typical, I'm told, of Tokyo weather during the late spring rainy season. As soon as I'm off the plane, many dark-blue-suited Japanese businessmen talking on their keitai surround me in the terminal. "*Hai, hai,*" they respond as they bow to what I imagine to be an autocratic boss on the other end of the cell phone connection.

On the one-and-a-half-hour train ride from Narita to Tokyo, I get my first glimpse of Japan: in the late afternoon mist, a man tending the rice paddy is smaller in comparison to his surroundings. It is not that the man himself is smaller, nor are his surroundings larger. The way the man fits into his surroundings seems different but also familiar. What I see looks like the *ukiyo-e* woodblock prints I have seen in museums and art books. It is as if I have somehow entered the scale, the perspective, of Hokusai's and Hiroshige's Floating World.

As I look from the paddy to the hills, I notice the tops of Japanese hills are more pointed here. The many different shades of green in the grass and trees are more distinct in the gray of the afternoon: lime, emerald, olive, ivy, greens with tints of blue, of yellow, even a green as dark as the billiard-table green of my left-behind bedroom walls.

Arriving at Tokyo Station, I make my way through what is the largest and busiest train station in which I have ever been. Wide lines of people surge every which way. Countless signs, some even in English or a version that resembles English, direct passengers to color-coded subway lines, commuter lines, *shinkansen* lines, as well as to the seemingly endless number of station exits.

How much easier this would be with Ian, who is more comfortable in a bordering-on-chaos crowd. Pausing amid all the constant motion,

I finally find a sign with a symbol of a taxi. As I make my way in the direction the arrow seems to be pointing, I play over and over in my head the short phrase I learned, "*Roppongi kudasai*," which will supposedly politely tell the taxi driver the area of Tokyo where I want to go.

Making my way toward what I hope will be the correct exit, I check in my pocket for the copy of the Japanese map e-mailed to me by the International House, where I'll be staying until my apartment is ready in two days. "You should hand this map to the taxi driver," the accompanying message said. "Addresses are very difficult to find in Tokyo, and in the rest of Japan."

Surprisingly, all works as it should and the taxi drops me off at the International House, where, after checking in, I fall asleep in the single bed in my small, narrow room.

The next morning I get instructions from the cultural office at the I-House of where to get my very own *keitai* and order my *meishi*, name cards, two essentials to navigating life successfully in Japan.

Walking in Roppongi, my mind and body are lit up like the countless neon lights, which here in Tokyo are vertical. Signs in kanji, hiragana, and katakana, the three distinct pictorial and glyphic systems that comprise modern Japanese, as well as rōmaji (English letters), hang at every sight level:

> Cherry Cat
> Exciting Plaza
> Poet Box

What do these signs mean?

Roaming the winding alleys, I notice the electrical poles and wires that line the narrow streets. I wonder how secure they would be during an earthquake or a typhoon. Many fires and natural disasters have devastated Tokyo. Impermanence seems closer to the surface here.

Inundated by so many unfamiliar sounds and images, will I remember my way back to the I-House? Tokyo might be the only city in the world where you can make a right, another right, another right, and another right and not end up in the same place as you began.

Foreigners unfamiliar with Japanese customs often startle their hosts by walking into a home without taking off their shoes.

I don't want to be one of those foreigners, but the custom of removing shoes is problematic for someone like me. Japanese remove their shoes upon arrival and, when departing, put them back on with ease while standing. Because of my differently shaped feet—I was born missing bones in both of my legs—I need specially designed orthopedic shoes, as well as a cane, to get around. And even if I could manage around the house without them, I need to sit down to be able to take off and put on my bulky, differently shaped shoes. Without a chair in the *genkan*, the entranceway, I must, however ungracefully, sit down on the floor.

When I move into my Meijirodai apartment, I am relieved to see the *genkan* has a step high enough to sit down comfortably and take off my shoes when I enter and put on my shoes when I leave. I am also relieved that I am able to walk without shoes around my narrow two-room thinly carpeted Tokyo apartment mostly pain free.

When Eiko-san, my landlady, comes over to see why my cable modem isn't working, she says "*Shitsurei shimasu*" after taking off her shoes and stepping up into the apartment.

Then I notice all Japanese visitors, including the cable company men who come to see what's wrong with my Internet connection, all say this phrase as they enter.

Brenda, a Japanese American poet from New York and fellow grant recipient, lives upstairs. She has already been here for four months and knows some Japanese. I ask her about the phrase.

"It literally means the person is sorry, or embarrassed, they are about to commit a wrongful act," she explains.

"Embarrassed? Wrongful? All they are doing is taking off their shoes and entering my apartment, which I've invited them to do."

"Welcome to Japan."

I am far from the first foreign writer to make his way to Japan. Without Ian, my expected company, I must find new companions. The first of these is the work of American expatriate Donald Richie, who has lived in Tokyo since 1947. Through his writing, Richie introduced the West to much of modern Japanese culture, especially Japanese film. By reading Richie, I learn about Lafcadio Hearn. Richie and Hearn serve not only as guides but also as models of how a foreigner becomes intimate with Japan.

Hearn, born of a Greek father and an Irish mother, came to Japan from New Orleans, where he was a journalist. Early in 1890, *Harper's* offered Hearn, then a year younger than I am now, a trip to Japan to write about his experiences in the famously quaint and picturesque land. Upon arrival, Hearn searched for remnants of Edo-period Japan, the era of the shogun, the Japan that denied access to all but a few Portuguese and Dutch merchants. Hearn's search eventually led him to resurrect and re-create old Japanese tales, popularizing them not only abroad but also in Japan.

Donald Richie describes Lafcadio Hearn as "a short man. . . . The Japanese were then a short people. And, though he was not in the Western sense an attractive-looking person, in Japan few knew how foreigners were supposed to look."

Preparing to come to Japan, I promised myself I would take advantage of every opportunity that presented itself, that I would follow every lead I could possibly follow.

But right now, I have no leads. Besides Ototake Hirotada's memoir *No One's Perfect*, there is not much about disabled Japanese that has been translated into English. I contact Ototake's agent. I am rebuffed after one e-mail: "Ototake-san doesn't want to talk about being disabled, he wants to be a sportswriter."

Instead, I explore my new neighborhood. On the small shopping street nearby, I discover the corner stand hawking roast chicken breasts, potato croquettes, and assorted fried and boiled Japanese side dishes. The street seems not to have changed much since the Edo period. There are two short, squat elderly women, dressed in loose-fitting one-piece housedresses, cotton scarves wound around their heads. Every day they sit outside a ground-floor apartment seemingly more dilapidated than the other low-rise buildings on the street. Passing by, I often look into what I assume to be their apartment: nothing but chaotic piles of things they must have kept for countless years. I quickly avert my eyes.

When I first walk down the street, these women stare at me.

"Who are those women who are always sitting outside on the shopping street?" I ask Brenda.

"Aren't they wild?" Brenda says. "They stare at me all the time," she adds, "like all the shopkeepers stared at first. They were flustered when I first arrived and I couldn't speak any Japanese. They were afraid they wouldn't be able to help me because they couldn't understand me."

Perhaps the two women stared at me not because I am disabled but because I am new to the neighborhood, and because I am a *gaijin*, a foreigner? This is something I had never thought of before.

After leaving Brenda, I send an e-mail to ask Ian what he thinks of this. I also ask if he will visit me in Japan. Back in the U.S., it is the middle of the night. It will take him awhile to respond.

In the late afternoon, I spend time in Shin-Edogawa Koen, a small garden at the end of my street. Eiko-san says the poet Bashō wrote about this garden, but I am unable to locate the writing. The garden is home to a strange kind of bird, seemingly part pheasant, part duck, part wild turkey that squawks at me as I approach.

At dusk I often walk along the shallow Edogawa, more a canal than a river, across from the garden. This evening is a milky dusk; everything blends with the increasingly darker grayish-blue sky. Though the soon-to-be-night sky seems clear, the humidity makes it seem as if a mist envelopes the canal. All perspective vanishes. This is the "atmospheric limpidity" of which Hearn writes upon his arrival in Japan. Everything near and everything distant is sharply focused.

Leaning on the metal balustrade along the river, I realize it has never been so clear how I have internalized everything the world threw my way about my different body to the point where the feelings seemed my own. In Japan if people stare at me, it is because I am a *gaijin*. Here, where people keep their feelings about my disability to themselves and do not accost me on the street, my experience of being different has in a short time already contradicted my worst fears and expectations.

Walking back to my apartment, I think of Ian, about how I buy him a souvenir and postcard everywhere I go. But now, there is no refuge, no relationship waiting for me at home. My life is here, walking the streets of my Tokyo neighborhood, a single man.

After taking off my shoes in the *genkan*, I look at my apartment: the kitchen counter, the kitchen sink, the bathroom sink, the bathroom mirror—are all easily managed, unlike the too-high counters and sinks in my American house. I think how the tiny unit bathroom, with one source of water for both shower and sink, is so small that Ian would not fit in it.

Here in Tokyo the space doesn't feel small. I think of all the things I own back in Massachusetts: the twenty bookcases filled with books, the files with manuscript drafts and correspondence, paintings from ex-boyfriends, a collection of Balinese art, my eighty Pikachus. Here, I feel unencumbered.

The clock ticks loudly. Back home, I couldn't sleep, read, or even talk on the phone if I heard a clock ticking this loudly. The street traffic and distant highway noise kept me awake. Here in Tokyo I ignore the ticking of a clock. Traffic no longer disturbs me.

Before arriving in Japan, I wondered what my Tokyo nights would be like. I made sure my new laptop had DVD capability, so I could spend what I imagined would be lonely nights watching movies.

Now it is time to get ready for a night out, my first exploration of Tokyo gay bars. I sit on my single bed. Changing my clothes, I know it has been eighteen years since I was last single. It has been at least as long since I went to a bar alone.

Japanese gay bars are much smaller than those in most Western cities. GB, where Japanese go to meet *gaijin*, and vice versa, consists of a square bar ringed with stools. On each of the bar's four walls are more stools in front of a shallow ledge on which drinks can be placed. Photos of Hollywood movie stars—I identify Cary Grant and James Dean—adorn the walls, and in each of the four corners is a small TV screen playing music videos of unfamiliar pop stars with whom I'm sure Ian is familiar.

It is a Tuesday night so the bar is not crowded. Most of the stools are vacant. But there is a middle-aged, ruddy-faced, square-jawed Western man sitting next to me. Next to him stands a younger Japanese who wears small, round glasses. He is holding a large, fully stuffed manila envelope with both hands. I listen to their English conversation.

"What's in the envelope?" The Western guy's accent is Australian.

"Payroll," the man with the envelope answers. "I work for the financial department at my company and I'm in charge of depositing payroll."

"You're carrying the payroll with you to a bar in Nichōme?"

"Is it not normal to carry payroll to the bank?"

"You think that's funny?" I realize the Australian is talking to me. Had I laughed out loud? "Are you married?"

"Married?" I'd never been asked this in a gay bar before.

"The ring on your left hand." He calls my attention to the ring Ian gave me when we were in Bali, which I still wear. "There are lots of married guys here. But they're usually Japanese."

"I'm not married. It's a ring from my—" I pause. I don't know what to call Ian. "Ex." I've never used this to describe him before.

"I'm Allan."

"Australian?"

"How'd you guess?"

By the time I state the obvious, Allan has turned his attention to another young Japanese at his side.

Two

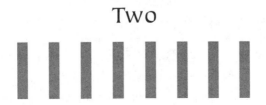

Fortune

Lafcadio Hearn avoided the world of luxury travelers and Christian missionaries. Instead, he enjoyed rickshaw rides into the back streets, delighting in the Yokohama hillside. But he constantly confronted the modernity that was rapidly consuming the older Japanese ways: "a shop of American sewing-machines next to the shop of a maker of Buddhist images; the establishment of a photographer beside the establishment of a manufacturer of straw sandals."

Though tempted at times by the cheap objects he found, Hearn quickly realized "the largest steamer that crosses the Pacific could not contain what you wish to purchase. For, although you may not, perhaps, confess the fact to yourself, what you really want to buy is not the contents of a shop; you want the shop and the shopkeeper, and streets of shops with their draperies and their habitants, the whole city and the bay and the mountains begirdling it, and Fujiyama's white witchery overhanging it in the speckless sky, all Japan, in very truth, with its magical trees and luminous atmosphere, with all its cities and towns and temples, and forty millions of the most lovable people in the universe."

A colleague at the Society for Disability Studies sends me an e-mail telling me to contact Nagase Osamu, a disability studies professor teaching at the University of Tokyo (Todai). Immediately, I contact Nagase and receive his reply asking to meet me.

Since I am, as usual, early to meet Nagase, I take a detour: this morning I follow the wide, raised, yellow plastic strips, familiar in Tokyo subways. But here the yellow plastic strips not only lead out into the streets but also continue a distance past the station. I have noticed, and tripped over, these plastic yellow paths inside the subways, but until this morning, I never noticed them outside before, and I never understood what they are for.

I follow the prefab "Yellow Brick Road" out of the station, across the main street, and up a slight incline along a side street. I turn a corner and find myself in front of the Library for the Blind.

Later, I mention the paths to Nagase.

"The yellow roads let the blind know how to get to the train tracks and where the platform ends so they don't fall in," he says.

"But the raised yellow paths make it more difficult for those who use wheelchairs or those who, like me, have difficulty walking on uneven surfaces," I reply.

"We are going to have a lot to talk about." Nagase tells me about Hanada Shuncho, a disabilities studies scholar who has cerebral palsy. He mentions Hanada-sensei's "Ebisu Mandala." The article describes Ebisu, one of the *shichifukujin*, the Seven Lucky Gods, as having cerebral palsy.

"A disabled god?" I ask. I have never before heard of a disabled Japanese god. "Shinto? Buddhist?"

"Kind of both. Or neither."

I wait for him to tell me more, but instead he asks, "Do you want to meet Fukushima-sensei and the research staff of our Barrier-Free Project?"

I want to know more about Ebisu. But I should answer his question. "Of course I do."

Nagase gives me articles about and by Fukushima Satoshi, a deaf-blind Tokyo University professor who runs Todai's Barrier-Free Project. He calls the project's secretary on his *keitai* and sets up a meeting.

Ebisu, a disabled god? I e-mail Nagase to find out more. In his response he provides a website address. I try to load the page. All I get is an error message.

Online, I do learn there is Ebisu, one of the Seven Lucky Gods, as well as the popular Ebisu beer. I can't find anything about Ebisu having cerebral palsy. I can't even figure out to what religion Ebisu belongs.

Many Asian cultures see disability from the Buddhist point of view: the result of having done something wrong in a previous life.

What might Buddhism tell me about how the Japanese view disability? I continue my search for Ebisu on the other side of Tokyo, at Sensō-ji, Tokyo's oldest Buddhist temple. Sensō-ji is in Asakusa, just west of the Sumida River in *shitamachi*, the "old town" part of the city. Most of this part of Tokyo, including most of the venerated temple, was destroyed during the war.

As soon as I pass through a vermillion gate and its imposing depictions of the white-faced god of thunder and the red-faced god of wind, I am swept up in the carnival atmosphere of the 250-meter-long Nakamise, the lantern-adorned arcade leading to the temple. Countless small shops from which I buy souvenirs and sweets line the way. All is color and excess bordering on "kitsch," for which there is no Japanese word.

I pass through another towering double-storied gate, this one displaying two enormous straw replicas of the Buddha's sandals.

I hear the sound of wood against metal but cannot locate its origin.

But there's smoke wafting from a large cauldron. Surrounding the cauldron, worshippers fan the smoke toward their faces. I look over the cauldron's rim: inside are numerous incense wands standing in what seems to be gray, ash-like sand. The smoke enshrouds the steep, long flight of stairs to the orange-red and gilded-gold *hondo*.

The energy outside in the Nakamise is matched by the raucous bustle inside the cavernous *hondo*, the main temple hall. The wall paintings of the life of the Buddha are cacophonous not only in their colors but in their numerous depictions of Buddhist deities. But, as far as I can tell, there is still no sign of Ebisu. Sensō-ji's main devotional object is a *hibutsu*, an image of a tiny Kannon too holy to be on view. I'm frustrated, as well as intrigued, by what I cannot see.

In front of the main altar, I remember what I read in my guidebook: I bow twice, close my eyes, clap twice, bow once more. I leave my first prayers in Japan—for Ian to visit me—inside the hall.

At the top of the *hondo* stairs, I look out over the smoking cauldron and the Nakamise. I have seen this view before. But in the famous Hiroshige print in his Famous Sights of Edo series, this view includes a large red festival lantern. I remember that Asakusa was once Tokyo's Yoshiwara, its pleasure quarters, where geisha and Kabuki actors entertained the growing middle classes of late Edo-period Tokyo. I am standing amid what was once The Floating World.

Descending the stairs, I finally locate the origin of the sound of wood hitting metal. Along the path to the temple are the famous Sensō-ji fortunes: bamboo sticks in a silver container. I pay one hundred yen and am handed a container. I shake it. One wooden stick escapes from the small hole on one end of the rectangular box. On the edge of the stick are kanji. Each combination of kanji matches with one of the array of drawers lining the entry walk to the temple. Each drawer contains a fortune.

The kanji are worn away from use. The characters on my stick are difficult to match with its drawer.

At last, I am able to find the proper drawer. I open the drawer and remove the small white paper on which is written—one side in Japanese, one side in English—No. 48 Small Fortune:

Just like looking at the treasure of other people beyond the valley. Let's stop to hurt your heart and give trouble to your mind.

If once a chance comes you can meet an excellent fortune. Just like a giant happy bird fly up to sky, you will succeed in this society, and rise to be famous in the world, meeting with so many fortunes.

*If you have right mind, your request will be granted later on. *The patient, the sickness may last long, but is sure to get well. *The lost article will be found. *The person you wait for will come late. *Building a new house and removal might have a little trouble at first but it get well later. *Marriage, employment and to start a trip are all half good fortune.

I'm disappointed by this fortune, which seems neither good nor bad. It doesn't give me any true direction.

Direction? Before arriving in Japan, I would not have even paid attention to a paper fortune pulled from a metal box at a temple for a religion I hardly understand. But I am worried by the sickness that may last. And I am stung by what the fortune says about wanting to stop to hurt my heart and give trouble to my mind. Is it Ian who is hurting my heart? He has yet to respond to my e-mail asking if he has booked his flight to Japan. Or is it my fruitless search for Ebisu—he doesn't seem to be Buddhist—giving trouble to my mind?

If you have right mind, your request will be granted later on.

Is my request the same as my prayer?

More important: what is the right mind?

In Japan my questions don't seem to get me anywhere, but I don't seem able to stop asking so many questions. If I'm unable to stop questioning, then at least I can postpone the need to find the answer until later. In this way, I can, like Donald Richie writes, "truly observe. Observation, appreciation, and through these, understanding."

I notice the many twisted strips of paper tied to a metal wire. Should

I keep my paper fortune with me or leave it behind with the countless others?

Brenda accompanies me to the annual reception of the foundation that is supporting us in Japan.

At the reception the staff keeps introducing me to the guests. Each person to whom I am introduced hands me his or her *meishi*, and I give each mine. I remember not to put someone's *meishi* away while we are talking, refraining from slipping them in my pocket until the conversation is over and the person I was talking to has moved on. By the end of the evening, I have a thick stack of *meishi* in my shirt pocket.

It is late in the evening and I am on my way to the bathroom when I notice a widely smiling, short, rotund, bald Japanese man. He seems to be in his late fifties or early sixties and is wearing a tie with cartoon penguins on it.

"That's a great tie," I say to the man as I pass by.

"It is always a great icebreaker," the man says, focusing his wide smile on me. "I wear it to international conferences where many languages are spoken, and it always does the trick." He laughs heartily. "Muramatsu Masumi," he says, extending his hand. He gives me his *meishi*, which also has a penguin similar to the one on his tie. "But you can call me MM."

I present my *meishi* to MM and read his *meishi*, which tells me he is the founder and president of the English-Speaking Union of Japan.

MM reads my name from my *meishi*, pronouncing it correctly since the Japanese katakana characters are phonetic. "So, you are one of the artists being supported by the foundation. What is your business in Japan?"

"I am a writer researching disability in Japan."

"Disability. Is this the politically correct word? Is this the word that is now used?"

"It's the word I prefer. None are perfect."

"Yes, words can be like that."

"Others use words like *physically challenged* or the unfortunate *differently abled.*" I stop, realizing that what I had just said might be misunderstood. "I mean I find the choice of the phrase unfortunate, not the so-called differently abled."

MM roars his warm laughter. "Many years ago, we used to call our live-in housekeeper *jochu.* However, as time has passed the word developed pejorative—pejorative, is that the right word?—connotations, and we no longer use it. Interesting how the meaning of words can change over time. Is this the kind of work you do?"

"Kind of. It is something I think about."

"I would like to talk more with you about this and other subjects."

"I have your *meishi* and will call you."

"Please do. And when we meet, I will wear another interesting tie."

I bow my head slightly and make my way to the bathroom.

Naoko, on the staff, intercepts me. "Do you know who was talking with you?" she asks.

"He says to call him MM."

"Muramatsu-sensei is a famous man. He was the first simultaneous interpreter in Japan, interpreting for all important dignitaries. Presidents. Prime ministers. He also was the voice heard on Japan television speaking Neil Armstrong's famous lines when he landed on the moon."

MM and I begin meeting regularly for noodles. No matter where we go together, we somehow end up eating noodles. In Kanda, shopping for old books, he takes me to a famous old noodle restaurant. After seeing Kabuki, I take him to a noodle shop under the elevated train tracks near Ginza.

"How do you know these places?" one of us invariably asks the other when we are delighted to be eating noodles together again.

I have never had a friend like MM before. His love of different languages, different cultures, and different senses of humor—he is a connoisseur of international humor—is catching. He has traveled all over and met most of the world's leaders during the past four decades, and when he retired he was still the finest simultaneous interpreter in Japan. This seventy-one-year-old man, a year older than my father, has more energy than I do. He thrives on the Internet, constantly using his laptop to research and send e-mails as he travels.

During our time together, I begin to hear MM's story. Alone as a teenager living near Asakusa after the war (his family had escaped the Tokyo air raids for the countryside), he began collecting metal and bringing it to someone who manufactured toys. Soon, he was selling the toys. Then, he found a job as a clerk, typing for the occupying U.S. Army, which is how he first learned English. He studied at Waseda University in the evenings. In 1956 he moved with his wife to the U.S. to work for the Japan Trade Council, eventually becoming its director.

"Washington, DC, was a smaller city when I lived there," he tells me. "I was well known around town as the character who drove his Pontiac dressed in a *yukata*."

Returning to Japan in 1965, MM helped establish Simul International, which became the best-known school for interpreters in Japan.

MM asks me to speak to his English-Speaking Union. After my talk, he introduces me to many of his former students, invariably women younger than he, with whom he has kept in touch years after he was their teacher.

Eating noodles after the talk, I ask MM, "What do you know about Ebisu?"

"The beer?"

"The *shichifukujin*. Are they Shinto or Buddhist?"

"I think legend says they come from China. Have you heard of Lafcadio Hearn?"

"I've been reading about him ever since I knew I was coming to Japan. "

"Last year I was in Matsue, where Hearn once lived. There's a memorial hall, a museum, in his old house. I was outside the house when I started a conversation with a nice man. Turns out he was Hearn's great-grandson. He now runs the museum." MM lets out his boisterous laugh.

"It's a beautiful place with a small area still reminiscent of old Japan. I will take you there. In *Kwaidan,* Hearn tells the tale of Hōïchi, the earless blind *biwa* singer. It's a ghost story. I love ghost stories. We should go see the ghost stories this month at Kabuki-za."

"*Bakemono.*" I say the Japanese word for ghost or monster.

"Yes, ba-ke-mo-no," MM inimitably repeats, distinctly pronouncing each syllable, as if he wants to make sure I pronounce Japanese correctly. "*Bakemono* literally means a thing that changes."

Before Buddhism there was Shinto.

Shinto, the Imperial religion, "the way of the gods," received its name only in the sixth century to distinguish itself from Buddhism, which had recently arrived from China. In Shinto, *kami*, gods, are everywhere: present in nature and objects. There are Shinto ways of doing things. For over two thousand years, it has become an integral part of what it means to be Japanese.

Researching Shinto, I discover the Japanese word *misogi*, a ritual of all-encompassing purity. Purity seems to be important to Shinto. How might this relate to the Japanese view of disability?

Followers of Shinto, which is practically everyone in Japan, believe they are the children of both their parents and the *kami*. They owe their lives to both society and nature. In return for love and protection, they are obliged to treat both with loyalty and respect. According to Shinto belief, when Japanese die they become *kami*, so not only are their ancestors *kami* but they themselves will become *kami*, an unbreakable relationship down through the generations.

Is Ebisu a Shinto *kami*? To find out, I decide to visit Meiji Jingu, Tokyo's most venerated Shinto shrine. It is Sunday, the day when the teenage girls go to nearby Harajuku to dress up in elaborate, often cartoonish, outfits.

Arriving at Harajuku Station, I follow the crowd out of the station.

When I turn the corner onto the bridge leading to Meiji Jingu, I am stopped by what seems like hundreds of girls on the bridge, as well as a crowd of onlookers.

The style, if that's the right word for it, of the clothes worn by the teenagers is one I have never seen before. The dominant colors are black and white, with an occasional bright red thrown in for emphasis. Short skirts and high woolen socks; long dresses in heavy fabric (even though it is a hot humid Sunday in late May) with thick high-soled close-to-the-knee black boots; hair dyed magenta, purple, and the blackest possible black. Faces painted Kabuki-white with lips smeared midnight purple, accentuating the pinkish red of corners of eyes and the inside of open mouths. Bras and slips, all kinds of undergarments worn as overgarments. Not quite 1980s East Village Punk or 1990s Seattle Grunge; it is, and isn't, both Victorian England and Jazz Age Chicago. A hybrid? An amalgam? "Trad by mod"? Nostalgia with more than one foot in the future? It is as if many—too many?—past styles have been thrown together for no apparent reason other than it can be done.

I am both amazed and appalled—amazed at this burst of nonconformity in a culture of conformity; appalled, aesthetically at first, but after a while of watching, the nonconformity seems to follow a pattern, leading back to a kind of conformity, after all.

I pass over the bridge; everything is changed. The cityscape around the concrete bridge turns into dense, lush forest. The sign tells me 365 tree species, donated from all over Japan, line the wide path to the shrine.

I pass under the twelve-meter-high, over nine-meter-wide, cypress *torii*. I have entered sacred ground. Donald Richie writes: "Japan is entered; the event is marked, as one enters a Shinto shrine, by passing beneath the *torii* gateway. There is an outside; then, there is an inside. And once inside—the experience begins with a new awareness, a way of looking, a way of seeing."

Is this the beginning of a new way of seeing?

I am led by my senses. Walking close to the *torii*, I breathe in the 1,700-year-old cypress. I press my face against the wooden gate's smoothness. I have never felt wood so smooth.

To the side of the shrine entrance is the *temizusha*, the fountain where, following the directions of the English sign, I use the long bamboo dipper to pour water over one hand, then the next. I take a sip of the water, making sure my lips don't touch the dipper, as instructed: to purify.

Inside the main courtyard of the shrine, the low walls allow the eye to follow across the space to the *honden*. All is Japanese cypress and copper roofs rusted an ethereal pale green. I cross the courtyard, walk up the stairs to the *honden*, and notice a few more of the lightning-shaped strips of white paper hanging near the entrance. I hear a faint rhythmic drumbeat but cannot find from where the sound emanates.

In front of the altar, I throw a few ten-yen coins, hear them clatter to the bottom of the slatted wooden box of offerings. In my short time in Japan, I have now asked both Shinto and Buddhist deities, whoever they may be, for Ian to visit me.

But to whom or what am I praying? In the shrine there are no representations of a *kami* or Ebisu or any other divinity.

I came to Meiji Jingu for a practical reason: to learn if Ebisu belongs to Shinto. But what I have learned is not concrete, does not relate to Ebisu: what is unseen is just as, if not more, important than what is seen.

Nor does what I've learned relate to purity. Back at the entrance, I once again look across the courtyard at the shrine. I can think of only one word: *serenity*.

I breathe deeply and relax for the first time since I arrived in Japan.

Three

‖‖‖‖‖‖‖

Barrier Free

A computerized female voice recites the name of the train stop. Then, a short three-note jingle sounds.

Alone, as I ride the Tokyo subway, I repeat to myself what I hear as if I am listening to a language-learning tape. I learn how to pronounce Japanese by listening to the train announcements. But I do not know what the words mean.

And I don't understand any of the scroll-like ads dangling alongside the hold-on straps: smiling women's faces; phosphorescently cute mascot-like creatures; ethereal landscapes of placid rivers, cloudless blue skies, and snow-topped mountains.

Trying to discern what I see and hear, I am forced to depend on what I sense, not on what I understand.

Later, when I ask someone who knows Japanese what *mamonaku tsugiwa* means or what the advertisement with a turquoise turtle-like cartoon creature is selling, I still keep my imagined meaning in mind. What I imagine somehow seems, to me, more real.

In the days before my meeting at Todai's Barrier-Free Project, I find out as much as I can about Fukushima-sensei, the head of the project. He first became blind at the age of nine. "I wasn't too shocked because sound was still left for me, even if I lost my sight. However, when I shifted from the state of total blindness to the total deafblindness, an enormous shock overtook me."

Fukushima-sensei could no longer "cherish the beautiful scenery of the starlit sky or the sea at sunset." He "could no longer awake in the morning to the song of the birds that comes afloat through the open window or delight to the beautiful melody of Bach and Mozart that comes forth from the audio system." But what gave Fukushima-sensei the greatest pain was "not the loss of sight and hearing itself but the vanishing of communication with others."

Until he acquired the skills of touch-Braille, until his friends also acquired the skills, and until he received interpretation services, Fukushima-sensei despaired. But once all three were in place, he was once again able to enter the world of communication. In 1983, with this support, he was able to become the first deafblind person to study in a university in Japan. He studied pedagogy for deafblind children and continued these studies in graduate school before becoming a university professor, eventually holding his current job.

In the Todai conference room, I sit across from Fukushima-sensei. He is flanked by two interpreters. I notice the interpreter on Fukushima-sensei's left lightly holds his hand. Nagase tells me that one interpreter will translate my English into Japanese; the other will translate the Japanese into touch-Braille for Fukushima-sensei: "Everyone present who can hear can speak and understand English."

I nod my head slightly to show I understand.

It is Fukushima-sensei who speaks first, in Japanese. I wait for the interpreter to interpret: "Welcome to our office at the University of

Tokyo in Komaba. We are honored to have you with us and look forward
to learning about your research today. Nagase has told us about your
work in the United States and we thank him for arranging this important
meeting. We hope you can let your colleagues know about our work
here in Japan. Please have copies of my writings on the history of disability studies in Japan. These are papers I have given at conferences,
which are mentioned at the top of each paper."

A staff member hands me a sheaf of papers.

"*Arigato gozaimashita*," I thank Fukushima-sensei.

"You know some Japanese."

"*Sukoshi*." Very little.

When Fukushima-sensei is finished telling me about the history of
the project, he asks me to tell him about my work.

"I wrote my first poems about disability in 1988," I say. I've never
spoken abroad about my work before. I realize I need to speak slowly, to
wait for the interpreters to interpret, first into Japanese, then into touch-
Braille, before moving on.

"When finding a publisher for the poems, I was asked by an editor if
I'd be interested in writing my story as a memoir. I said I would do anything for money."

When this is interpreted for him, Fukushima-sensei laughs.

"Then, I began writing my book about Darwin, Wallace, and evolution, and I realized that my shoes were an apt metaphor for variation
and adaptation."

"Who is Wallace?" asks the research associate on my right.

I tell him about Alfred Russel Wallace, the often-forgotten co-
founder of the theory of natural selection, who was in the Spice Islands,
what is now Indonesia, when he wrote to Darwin about his evolutionary
theory of natural selection.

"I began to see the story of evolution as an example of the social model
of disability, how there is no such thing as 'normal,' how each of us
adapts to his environment." I look around the room at the rapt listeners.

"But there are many things I, as a blind person, cannot do," says the research associate to my right.

I know that in formal meetings, agreement and consensus are very important in Japan. Disagreement should be avoided in a public setting. But I want to find out from where his feeling of limitation comes. Is it something he actually experienced or has he internalized what society teaches?

Here, in my first formal meeting in Japan, I have a choice to make: to point out there is another way to think about what had just been said or to let the comment go and move on.

"I'm not sure about what was just said," I hear myself say, making sure to choose my words carefully and to avoid asking a direct personal question.

Then, I realize that Fukushima-sensei will not hear my actual words. My words will be translated—not once but twice—changing in nuance, context, and connotation, as they are transformed by the interpreters, first from English to Japanese, and then from Japanese to touch-Braille.

"Everyone has limitations," I continue. "It's just that society views some limitations differently, as being more important, more limiting, than others. Might thinking that disabled people are more limited than the nondisabled be something we internalize without looking at how true it is?"

I pause to make sure the interpreters have the chance to translate my carefully chosen words as accurately as possible. As the touch-Braille interpreter finishes her translation into Fukushima-sensei's hand, everyone is silent.

Finally, the translation is complete. Fukushima-sensei nods his head. "I think what Fries-sama says is not only correct but is an advantageous way of viewing things."

I exhale deeply, realizing I have, in this situation, made the best choice. Also, Fukushima-sensei used the honorific *sama* when referring to me.

I ask how the research staff, some of whom, like Nagase, are not disabled, became involved in disability studies and the project. Everyone but Nagase had previously been a personal aide to Fukushima-sensei. This surprises me.

"This is interesting. In the United States, there is usually a great educational and, most of the time, a class and/or racial divide between the disabled and their aides. Do you think this isn't the case here because Japan is a more homogenous society? Or is helping the disabled, like teaching for that matter, given more respect here in Japan than in the West?"

"That is a very good question for us to think about," Fukushima-sensei says. "We thank you very much for coming to see us today and having this very important discussion. Please let us know if there is anything we can do for you during your stay in Japan, and I want to read your new book when it is published."

I look at the clock: 1:00 p.m. Though we did not get to discuss, let alone answer, my question, it is time for the meeting to end.

In Japan this will not be the last time that my questions are not answered directly or not answered at all. Will my time in Japan be a series of unanswered questions?

One night, after MM and I finish eating noodles, he hands me a small green book: *Kwaidan: Stories and Studies of Strange Things*, by Lafcadio Hearn.

"*Domo arigato gozaimashita*," I thank MM both verbally and with a slight bow of my head.

Why did MM give me *Kwaidan*? I remember MM mentioning Hearn's story of Hōïchi, a blind *biwa hōshi*.

During the early history of Japan, blindness, often caused by disease, farming accidents, or poor nutrition, was very common. By the eighth century, blind storytellers roamed Japan, chanting narratives in exchange for alms. Accompanying themselves on the four-stringed fretted lute called a *biwa*, the *biwa hōshi* (lute priests) spread news, popular songs, and local legends.

Hōïchi lived in a temple near the Straits of Shimonoseki, where the last great battle between the Heike and the Taira clans was fought. One night, the head priest is called away and Hōïchi, left alone at the temple, hears someone calling him.

"I am blind!—I cannot know who calls!"

The voice tells him there is nothing to fear. His lord has heard of Hōïchi's skill in reciting. The voice orders him to come with him and perform for his lord.

After his performance in what seems to be a garden, a woman's voice tells him her lord desires Hōïchi to perform before him for the next six nights. He is warned to tell no one.

But on the second night, Hōïchi is discovered returning to the temple. The priest asks where he had gone. Hōïchi answers, "I had to attend to some private business; and I could not arrange the matter at any other hour."

The priest does not ask any further questions, but he fears that his blind acolyte had been "bewitched or deluded by some evil spirits."

So, on the third night, temple servants follow Hōïchi. But on this dark and rainy night, they lose him. Finally, in the cemetery, they hear the sound of the *biwa*. They discover Hōïchi sitting alone in the rain before a memorial tomb, loudly chanting of the battle of Dan-no-ura. Surrounding Hōïchi are "the fires of the dead . . . burning, like candles."

The temple servants laugh at him, seize him, and return him to the temple. Knowing he has alarmed and angered the priest, Hōïchi confesses what has happened.

The priest responds: "Hōïchi, my poor friend, you are now in great danger! . . . Your wonderful skill in music has indeed brought you into strange trouble. By this time you must be aware that you have been . . . passing your nights in the cemetery, among the tombs of the Heike. . . . All that you have been imagining was illusion—except the calling of the

dead. By once obeying them, you have put yourself in their power. If
you obey them again, after what has already occurred, they will tear you
in pieces."

The priest tells Hōïchi he will protect him by writing holy scriptures
on his body. With their writing-brushes, they trace the text of a holy
sutra on all parts of his body.

The priest tells Hōïchi to sit on the verandah and wait. When he is
called, he is not to answer and not to move. He should sit still, as if
meditating.

His *biwa* beside him, Hōïchi sits still on the verandah for many
hours.

Then, he hears steps coming. A voice in front of him calls his name.
Hōïchi does not answer.

The voice, now displeased, comes closer. "Here is the *biwa*; but of
the *biwa*-player I see—only two ears! . . . There is nothing left of him
but his ears. Now to my lord those ears I will take—in proof that the
august commands have been obeyed, so far as was possible."

Hōïchi feels an awful pain in his ears but does not cry out. The foot-
steps recede and then cease. Hōïchi feels on either side of his head a
warm trickling but dares not lift his hands.

The priest returns. He slips and cries out in horror. By his lantern's
light, he sees Hōïchi sitting in meditation, blood oozing from his wounds
and onto the floor.

Hearing the priest's voice, Hōïchi cries and tells the priest what has
transpired.

"Poor, poor Hōïchi," the priest exclaims, "all my fault! . . . Everywhere upon your body the holy texts had been written—except upon
your ears! I trusted my acolyte to do that part of the work; and it was
very, very wrong of me not to have made sure that he had done it! . . .
We can only try to heal your hurts as soon as possible. . . . The danger is
now well over. You will never again be troubled by those visitors."

Hōïchi soon recovers. The story of his adventure spreads throughout
Japan. The nobility travels to hear him recite; he receives many gifts and

becomes wealthy. From the time of his adventure, he becomes known as Mimi-nashi-Hōïchii, Hōïchi-the-Earless.

Hōïchi-the-Earless is the first disabled cultural icon I encounter in Japan. I am surprised that the familiar Western character of the blind seer, like Tiresias in *Oedipus Rex*, who has the means to negotiate between the seen and the unseen world, is also deeply rooted in Japan.

The next time I see MM, I tell him I read "Hōïchi-the-Earless."

"Did you know Hearn had only one eye?" MM asks.

"How did he lose an eye?"

"A playground fight as a child. In Japan nobody mentioned his face looked . . . twisted—is that the right word?"

Was Hearn's attraction to "strange things" because of having one eye?

In August 1890 Hearn abandoned his contract with *Harper's* and moved to Matsue, a traditional castle town on the Sea of Japan in the remote northwest corner of Honshu, the largest island of Japan, to teach at the boys' high school.

In Matsue, Hearn found "survivals" of an undisturbed old Japan. He taught by day and began cataloging the festivals and folkways of Matsue at night. He hired translators to provide him with literal translations of Japanese poems and folktales. He looked for *kokoro*, a Japanese word difficult to translate, best understood as "things of the heart," which could reveal to him the deep roots of Japan.

But what haunts me is Hōïchi's vulnerability. To Hōïchi, there is little to distinguish between the living and the dead.

Four

||||||||

Foreign Affairs

In the Edo-Tokyo Museum, I cross over the Nihonbashi Bridge, the famous bridge that was the terminus of the Tōkaidō highway, the road between Edo and Kyoto, the bridge from which the Japanese measured distances. But the bridge I cross over is the replica of the original wooden bridge.

From the bridge, I can see all the museum exhibits, displaying the history of Tokyo, below. I spot a thirtysomething Japanese man who leads a Western man who seems a bit older through the displays of old Japan. They stop in front of the model of the long-ago-destroyed Edo Castle. The *gaijin* lightly rests his palm on the lower back of his Japanese guide. He leans toward his companion and says something into his ear before they move on to another exhibit.

Following the couple through the museum, I wonder if I might find a Japanese man who shares my interests as much as Ian. What might it be like to have someone who could intimately guide me through this still-unfamiliar culture?

Brenda came to Japan to learn and write about her mother's Okinawan roots. She arrived with her girlfriend. A month later the relationship was over. She went to Okinawa but felt restricted by her Okinawan relatives. Back in Tokyo, Brenda stopped at a "live house," a small music venue. She was the only *gaijin*. She sat at the bar, wanting to practice her Japanese. But everyone at the bar wanted to practice speaking English.

Brenda noticed a band setting up to play. Specifically, she noticed a skinny, long-haired Japanese guy.

"When I first saw him, I knew he was going to be my husband," she tells me.

"Your husband? I thought you came to Japan with a woman."

"I did. But that's what I thought when I first saw him," she offers as an explanation. "I sat at the bar for the band's first set and practiced my introductory lines in Japanese. He didn't look like the type who spoke much English."

Between sets, Brenda introduced herself to the skinny band member with the long black hair.

"Did you tell him he was going to be your husband?"

"I told him I liked his playing. He said he'd talk to me after they stopped playing for the night."

I am impressed with Brenda being able to communicate with a non-English-speaking Japanese, something I can't imagine doing myself.

After the band stopped playing, while the band members packed up their stuff, Brenda waited at the bar. Taka—that was her future husband's name—finally came over.

Way after midnight, Taka walked Brenda to her apartment. At the small gate in front of the path that leads to both of our apartments, Taka said good night.

"He didn't even kiss me. Even though we exchanged *meishi*, I thought I'd never see him again."

Only later did Brenda learn that Taka didn't go with her into her apartment that night because she hadn't asked. Or so he told her when they began seeing each other regularly.

Brenda continues her tales of Taka by telling me how he never introduces her to any of his friends, he always calls to say he is on his way to see her, and he always shows up hours later.

"I spend most of my nights waiting for him. He always shows up. But I never know when."

Let's get out of here and get some food," Allan says, ushering me off my GB stool, through the bar, and into the narrow Nichōme streets. He leads me to a chain restaurant. "I come here for waffles," Allan says. He translates the different flavors. We order.

Sitting across from him, I notice Allan doesn't look so good. The ruddy face I remember is pale. He looks as if he hasn't slept well.

"Are you okay?" I ask.

"Last night I saw Yoshihiro for the first time in over seven years."

Of course, having met Allan only once before, and very briefly, I have no idea who Yoshihiro is.

"I met Yoshihiro at a small Nichōme bar. I was in Tokyo teaching— I've been teaching off and on in Tokyo for what must be twenty years now. I was married at the time. I was new to Japan, knew little Japanese. Yoshihiro knew little English. But he showed me his Tokyo. He had a fondness for cemeteries. Once, he took me to Aoyama Cemetery, and when we left he asked if I'd seen the *bakemono* on his shoulder. Yoshihiro always saw *bakemono*—it can't be translated into English so we just say *ghosts*. Yoshihiro was the most un-Western person I had ever known. But somehow, despite our different cultures, we developed an intimacy— a common space."

"Was Yoshihiro the first man you were with?"

Allan vigorously nods his head.

"What about your wife?"

"When I returned to Australia, it was a difficult divorce." Allan looks down and pauses. I notice his right hand is shaking. "After Yoshihiro's mother died, he came to Australia with his calligraphy materials and a small worn suitcase bound with rope. For years we shuttled back and forth from Melbourne to my frequent teaching stints in Tokyo. But I never realized, until it was too late, that Yoshihiro wanted me to sponsor him for permanent residency in Australia. Gradually, our visits, letters, and telephone calls dwindled, and then there was a long silence."

Allan pauses, then continues, "I visited Tokyo a couple of times, but my meetings with Yoshihiro were always hasty. We spent one night together, which was incredibly tender but also a kind of farewell. He told me I would always be his *special friend.*"

Allan stops as if contemplating the phrase he just said.

"I was teaching in Kobe during the 1995 earthquake. I was ill with the pneumonia that swept through Kobe and had no way to get to or communicate with Tokyo. Finally, a week after the earthquake, I was able to return to Tokyo. I met with Yoshihiro at one of our favorite restaurants. I had been through so much, needed his physical attention, and was so happy to see him. He sat across from me holding a small lacquer box. He opened the box and handed me money. 'What's this for?' I asked him. 'It's from my ancestral inheritance from my mother. Please use it to spend the night in a comfortable hotel.'"

Allan's head is raised. He looks past me.

"Here was my lover of over thirteen years telling me to spend the night of our reunion—I had been so sick and wanted to be with him—in a hotel. I stared at him and when I could stare no longer, I got up, left the money on the table, and walked out of the restaurant. I didn't see him again until last night."

Allan still doesn't look at me. "Feeling sick in Kobe was the first sign that I had cancer. I never heard from Yoshihiro. When I was sick in the hospital back in Australia, I would see Yoshihiro across the room watching me."

"What did you say to each other last night when you saw him?"

"He told me that he was irretrievably hurt by my rejection of his ancestral money. I told him that was not what I wanted—I wanted to spend the night with him, be held by him, to be loved by him, physically. He saw his gesture as a gift and sacrifice; I saw it as cold indifference. According to what he believed, he gave me what was most important to him, but it was not what I needed."

Allan closes his eyes. His face contorts as if he feels, somewhere in his body, a sharp pain.

After a long pause, Allan opens his eyes. Looking directly at me, he says, "The thing is, when I was so sick in Australia, I don't know if what I saw was a hallucination or his spirit, like the *bakemono* he often carried on his shoulder."

I sit on my narrow bed.

I call Ian. No answer.

I look at the ticking clock: not yet ten o'clock. Still early enough to see who is at GB tonight.

At the bar, I pay the 500-yen cover charge, order ginger ale as my included-in-the-cover-charge drink, and make my way to the opposite corner, from where I can see the entire bar as well as all the men who enter.

I am on my second ginger ale when I notice a very attractive blue-suited Japanese guy, maybe in his early thirties, looking at me. When he sees me look at him, he smiles. I am never sure when someone is interested in me. I nod my head slightly and smile back before I quickly look away.

A middle-aged man who does not seem Japanese sits next to me. To distract myself from the attractive blue-suited Japanese guy, I ask the man sitting next to me where he is from.

"Venezuela. But I've lived in Japan for the past five years. I'm Rafael. Where are you from? What are you doing in Tokyo?"

Somewhere between my answer that I am a writer researching a book and his asking me how long I am going to be in Tokyo, I look at the very attractive blue-suited guy who earlier had been looking at me and notice that he is now talking to a *gaijin* who had sat himself next to him at the bar. He sees me looking at him and, once again, smiles.

"I'll be here for six months," I tell Rafael.

As I talk with Rafael, I notice the *gaijin* is now touching the neck of the very attractive guy who—how long has it been?—had looked at me.

I guess nothing's going to happen with him, I think before realizing Rafael is waiting for my response to a question I did not hear. By the time the conversation with Rafael has run its course—he has to get home so he can be awake at work tomorrow—I realize the man who had been looking at me, as well as the *gaijin* who had been touching his neck, have left the bar. I am surprised by how disappointed I feel.

I check my *keitai* for the time: after midnight. I have probably missed the last train and will have to take a taxi to get home, which means I will have to remember the Japanese words—*hidari* is left, *migi* is right, or is it the other way around? I know *massugu* is straight ahead—I need to direct the taxi driver to my apartment. But even if I remember the words, will I remember the landmarks where the driver should turn?

I get down from my stool—always an interesting moment because, when seated, my disability isn't noticeable—and make my way toward the door, up the stairs, and into the narrow streets of Nichōme.

On the street, in front of the bar, is the very attractive guy.

"I've been waiting for you," he says, smiling.

Did he know I was disabled before I walked out of GB? I start to walk toward Shinjuku-dori, where I figure I can catch a taxi.

"Where are you going?"

"Back to my apartment, if I can remember how to get there. What happened to the guy who was touching your neck?"

"Ah, him, he's French." He laughs.

When we reach Shinjuku-dori, the attractive man draws me to him and kisses me.

Shinjuku-dori wa doko desu ka? As we kiss, the phrase I had practiced saying over and over again for months before departure, so I would remember how to ask where somewhere is, repeats in my head. I can't believe that here I am, on Shinjuku-dori, kissing this very attractive Japanese man.

"I can't take you to where I live," he says. "It's not prepared."

Not prepared? What does that mean? I ask, "Where can we go? The trains have stopped and I'm not sure I know how to get back to my place by taxi."

"There's a love hotel."

"A love hotel? Where?" I had read about Japan's love hotels, the places where lovers, both illicit and otherwise, go since there is little privacy, or space, in most Japanese homes.

"Just above the bar."

"That's convenient."

"Let me get some money. Stay here."

Was this an excuse to make his exit? Did I too easily let his tongue into my mouth? Did he not like the way I returned his kiss? Standing in the neon-lit Shinjuku-dori, did he finally realize I am only five feet tall? I wait. Not only because I'm unsure how to get back to my apartment. I want to know if the very attractive man actually went to get money.

In a few minutes, he returns, takes my hand, and leads me back down the narrow street. Just past the stairs to GB, he takes me into the dark empty lobby of what I assume is the love hotel. Two prices—one for "Rest," one for "Stay"—are listed in English.

"There's nobody here," I hear myself say.

"Don't worry, she'll come."

And the front door of the hotel opens and a voice says, "*Arigato gozaimashita*," which I know means *thank you*. I have accidentally stood on the carpet, which must activate the automatic door that is accompanied by what is by now a very familiar Japanese female computer voice.

Then, a door near the front desk opens and out comes a small, hunched-over elderly Japanese woman pulling a metal pail with a mop in it.

The very attractive guy pays the woman and leads me into the elevator, to the third floor, and into a room that is garishly lit by a mysterious green light emanating from what might be a television or a fish tank with no fish or some kind of see-through refrigerator door.

I sit down on a chair across from the bed as the very attractive guy starts to undress.

"I'm Masa," he says as he neatly folds and hangs up his clothes.

"Kenny," I say and figure I should take off my clothes, as well.

Masa comes to me in his boxers and pulls me toward the bed. He starts kissing me and much sooner than expected, I am on my back and Masa is lowering himself onto me.

"We need a condom," I tell him.

"Oh," he says.

"I have one."

He stays on top of me as I reach for my wallet.

"Wait a minute, I have to call downstairs."

My very rudimentary Japanese allows me to catch something he says about 8:00 a.m. I realize Masa and I are not going to rest. We are going to stay the night at the love hotel.

Five

Mono no Aware

Among the papers given to me at the meeting with Todai's Barrier-Free Project is Nagase's English translation of his essay in his Japanese disability studies reader, a short history of the disability rights movement in Japan.

On May 29, 1970, in Yokohama, a thirty-one-year-old mother of three children, two with cerebral palsy, sent her two boys to bed at 10:00 p.m. But the daughter, whose disability was more severe and was usually confined to her bed, began to cry at midnight. She didn't stop crying. All day, the mother had been irritated by having so much to do to take care of her children. Her husband was away on a business trip. She became angry with her daughter and strangled her to death.

The newspaper reported that the mother had tried to find an institution to take her daughter, but there was no vacancy. A neighbor said the mother "loves her daughter so much, I wonder if Kiko [the daughter] should be put into a sanatorium because her symptoms do not improve." The newspapers quoted the mother: "Because she cried at night, I got angry with her, and killed her with my apron strings."

When the mother was arrested for murder, her neighbors collected seven hundred signatures, petitioning the authorities to allow the mother to return home. Sympathy for the mother and requests for court leniency by family organizations were widespread, the usual response when a case like this became public. Even though the mother was sentenced to two years in prison, the presiding judge said, "We should not distinguish a child with a disability from a normal child, but the defendant is suffering from mental fatigue and her husband was on a business trip. After consideration, I gave her a reprieve."

During the case, something unprecedented happened. Aoi Shiba (literally meaning "blue grass"), an organization of people with cerebral palsy, strongly and publicly protested against these sympathetic views.

I tell Nagase I am interested in meeting former Aoi Shiba members. "Not worth your time," he replies. "It happened a long time ago."

Remembering that in Japan even *maybe* means *no*, I let it go.

I meet Masa at the waffle restaurant. He tells me he is a Berklee College of Music trained pianist. He lives in an upscale area of Tokyo with his parents, who own the building in which they live. I also find out he has a boyfriend in Boston, where he often spends months at a time. He will go to Boston next week.

Leaving Masa, I'm surprised at how disappointed I feel. I did not know he already had a boyfriend.

To clear my head, I return to Meiji Jingu. This time, after passing through the tall cypress *torii*, knowing that by the middle of June the famous Meiji Jingu irises should be in bloom, I detour left.

I pass the empress's lotus-filled fishing pond and continue down a tree-lined path.

I turn the corner.

The marsh of irises, thousands of them in staggered rows, undulates in front of me: a violet profusion, every imaginable shade of purple. All this vivid color—too much color—stops me.

I do not know how long I stand looking at the marsh of irises.

Finally, I am able to cross the wooden bridge. I bend down to take a closer look. Only then do I notice other colors—the pinks, yellows, and blues comprising each distinct iris.

Before arriving in Japan, I had not written a poem in almost five years. After my mid-June visit to the Meiji Jingu iris garden, I start writing short six-line poems about Japanese gardens.

Although I am glad to be writing poems again, I am embarrassed at what I think of as the poems' "Orientalism." Here I am, a Westerner in Japan for only six weeks, and I am writing these compressed imagistic poems so similar to haiku. And to top it off, these poems are about Japanese gardens!

My disability research is stalled. Ebisu remains elusive. Masa is in Boston visiting his boyfriend.

I immerse myself in writing about Japanese gardens. Initially, I wanted to save visiting Kyoto for when Ian would be in Japan. But he has yet to tell me he will be visiting. I decide not to wait. Before the summer's humidity increases, I will go to Kyoto alone.

I learn as much as I can about Japanese gardens. I keep reading about *mono no aware*. To noted translator Sam Hamill, *mono no aware* is "a resonance found in nature . . . a natural poignancy in the beauty of temporal things. . . . *Aware* originally meant simply emotion initiated by the engagement of the senses." Ivan Morris, in his study of *The Tale of Genji*, says *aware* refers to "the emotional quality inherent in objects, people, nature, and . . . a person's internal response to emotional aspects of the external world." Donald Richie writes, "The awareness is highly self-conscious, and what moves me is, in part, the awareness of being moved, and the mundane quality of the things doing the moving."

My guidebook's photo of Kyoto's famous garden at Ryōan-ji shows some small pebbles in three divided sections. This confuses me. Could this be a garden? It looks more like a close-up of carefully arranged spices in a kitchen cupboard.

Hearn, in "In a Japanese Garden," writes:

Now, a Japanese garden is not a flower garden; neither is it made for cultivating plants. In nine cases out of ten there is nothing in it resembling a flower bed. Some gardens may contain scarcely a sprig of green; some have nothing green at all, and consist entirely of rocks and pebbles and sand. . . . In order to comprehend the beauty of a Japanese garden it is necessary to understand—or at least to learn to understand—the beauty of stones. Not of stones quarried by the hand of man, but of stones shaped by nature only. Until you can feel, and keenly feel, that stones have character, that stones have tones and values, the whole artistic meaning of a Japanese garden cannot be revealed to you.

The rock garden at Ryōan-ji is small, only thirty feet deep and seventy-eight feet wide. It consists of fifteen rocks, each of different size, color, and texture, placed in five groupings, surrounded by a sea of finely raked grayish-white sand. Viewed from the veranda of the monk's quarters, the garden is surrounded on its other three sides by a clay wall. The wall might have once been pale white but now is light rust and contains chance patterns; over many years the wall has been stained by oil.

From no one point can all fifteen rocks be seen. No matter where one sits, only fourteen rocks, at most, can be seen at one time. I notice a group of students counting the rocks. My eyes move from the students back to the rocks, first alighting on one group, then another, and then I become fixated on the Tàpies-like pattern on the oil-stained wall.

Looking at the garden, what seems like foreground becomes background; background becomes foreground. The wall is most prominent; then one of the rock groupings, or a single rock; then focus is on the raked sand. I realize why the guidebook photo is a close-up of a tiny corner edge of the garden: it is impossible to see all at once; the experience of Ryōan-ji is cumulative.

How long have I been here sitting here, looking?

How can something so still—so permanent—be, at the same, just as evanescent?

Although many have interpreted the meaning of the garden—a representation of islands in an ocean, some famous mountains from ancient Chinese texts, a tiger chasing its cub, a symbol for the Buddhist principle of unknowing—I have not ventured to interpret the garden beyond the experience of my viewing.

I get up and walk around to the other side of the monks' quarters. I bend down to get a closer look at the *tsukubai*, the stone water basin, on which there are four chiseled Japanese characters. The sign says that reading clockwise, including the hole in the middle of the water-filled basin, the characters mean "I learn only to be contented."

The tour of Shugakuin Rikyu, on the other side of Kyoto, is in Japanese. I am the only *gaijin* on the tour, the only person who does not understand or speak Japanese.

Shugakuin Rikyu covers a large area; there are three levels, each with its own garden and a distinctly different design. The two lower gardens are small and enclosed: ponds, a stream, waterfalls, stones, lanterns designed around spare wood imperial-style villas.

At the entrance to the upper garden, a path to the right rises through a hedge-covered stone stairway.

"*Daijoubu desu ka? Daijoubu?*"—"Are you okay? Is it okay?"—my fellow tourists keep asking me as we climb the stone path.

"*Daijoubu, daijoubu*, I'm okay, I'm okay," I assure them.

With the obstruction of the hedge, there is no view of the garden before ascent. However, once Rinuntei, the teahouse at the top of the stairs, is reached, the garden below—the clear pond reflecting all the garden's pines and maple trees, another teahouse, the two bridges leading across islands to the pond's other shore—can be seen. All of this is framed by the surrounding mountains, including the sacred Mount Hiei, not belonging to the garden but part of it, from which it is said the garden's pond, which also reflects the mountains as well as its streams and waterfalls, is fed.

This is my first experience of *shakkei*, the principle of "borrowed scenery": the surrounding landscape becomes part of the garden. This does not mean placing the garden so it has beautiful scenery nearby but actually incorporating shapes and textures of the surrounding landscape, and repeating those elements, as part of the garden itself. It is, Donald Richie writes, as if "the hand of the Japanese reaches out and enhances (appropriates) all that is most distant. Anything out there can become nature. The world is one, a seamless whole, for those who can see it."

At Shugakuin Rikyu, the hedge that at first seemed just a hedge is still a hedge. But the placement of the hedge, its purpose, unknown at first encounter, is only revealed at the right moment, heightening the experience of revelation. The view of the entire garden is delayed for maximum impact, delayed until it can be seen as "a seamless whole."

I once again think about my Senso-ji fortune: *If you have right mind, your request will be granted later on.*

I am impatient. When will the later on, the moment when I have right mind, be?

Do I need to change my request? Is it better to remain single? Should I forget about Ian visiting Japan?

Then, will I be one who can see "the seamless whole"?

A bodhisattva can achieve enlightenment but decides to stay on earth to assist others in achieving nirvana.

Kyoto's Kiyomizu-dera is said to have been constructed in 778 by Enchin, a Buddhist priest, in honor of the Kannon Bosatsu, bodhisattva of mercy and compassion. Built on a wooded hill in the eastern part of the city, the temple's *hondo* has a large outdoor wooden terrace. Just inside the *hondo*, I ring the large bronze bell. The ring echoes throughout the hillside and valley.

Below the terrace, down a long, steep stairway, is the Otawa-no-taki, the waterfall of pure spring water, which gives the temple its name. The water is said to have healing powers. Visitors line up to drink the water, catching the stream with long metal poles at the end of which is a cup.

But what am I trying to heal?

After I drink from the waterfall, I look up at the temple. I see the immense wooden crisscrossed girding that holds in place, hopefully less precariously than it looks, the *hondo*'s wide terrace high up on the adjoining hill.

Behind and up a short flight of stairs from the *hondo* is the Shinto Jishu Shrine, popular with lovers since it is believed the god of love and good marriages lives at the shrine. Like the Nakamise at Sensō-ji, the atmosphere of Shinto Jishu is surprisingly boisterous.

In front of the shrine are two rocks, placed several meters apart. Successfully walking from one rock to the other with your eyes closed is said to bring luck in love: if there is a particular person in mind, then successfully navigating from rock to rock ensures the relationship with that person will endure.

Those who walk between the rocks are laughing. Those watching are laughing, too. Some onlookers shout what I assume are encouraging words. Not knowing Japanese, I do not know if any of the called-out words would actually help those on their quest.

Watching the crowd, I think I should leave. I have already gotten from Kyoto what I came for: two more garden poems.

But I am caught up in the excitement. I find myself next in line.

I am nervous to try making my way from rock to rock with my eyes closed. My Sensō-ji fortune told me: *the person you wait for will come late*. Being single, who should I think of?

I close my eyes. Walking from rock to rock, I think of Ian.

My last night in Kyoto, I fall under the spell of Noh.

Donald Richie writes, "In Noh, natural forces, natural surroundings, are everything—it is an animistic theater, the theater of pure Shinto."

But what I see does not seem natural: an austere wood platform. A wooden shrine-like roof, reminiscent of what I've seen at Shinto shrines, covers the platform. On the back wall is a painting of a large, stylized pine tree shaped like the pine trees I've seen in the Kyoto gardens.

A kimono-clad actor enters the stage from a side walkway connected to the main platform. As he shuffles to the center of the stage, I notice the elaborate, ochre kimono, ornately embroidered with off-white flowers and leaves. The actor wears a white mask. The pale red lips of the mask are slightly open. The eyes of the mask are closed. It is as if the character the actor plays is in a deep sleep, dreaming.

But I know the character on stage is not dreaming. He is Semimaru, the most famous blind *biwa hōshi*. I have come to see the Noh play that bears his name.

Four musicians—three percussionists and a wooden flute player— have entered from a hidden door on the side of the stage. The music they play is all pulsing rhythm, with no discernable melody. Semimaru chants to the music, a garbled low-pitched chant.

He is joined by another masked character, this one with long, straggly hair, who has slowly glided onto the stage. I don't know what Semimaru and the long-haired character are saying to each other. Not even the Japanese could understand what is being chanted. But the aura the chanting creates reminds me of the sounds emitted by the old men who prayed in my childhood synagogue.

And now Semimaru is dancing. But a Noh dance is not like any dance I've ever seen. The movement starts very slowly. The fan held in Semimaru's left hand arcs downward; the foot, in a white *tabi* sock, flexes upward. The other foot stamps on the wood stage, a counter-rhythm to the percussive music.

After a long, screeching note from the high-pitched flute, dance completed, Semimaru shuffles off in the same direction—more quickly than he came.

The polite Japanese applause tells me the play is over.

What happened to the character with the long, straggly hair?

Has Semimaru died? Has he gone to heaven?

I have little understanding of what just transpired. But what I feel makes me wonder if my face looks like Semimaru's mask. It is as if time had been suspended and I can't tell if I had been awake or asleep.

Back at the hotel, I search for information that might explain what I had experienced watching *Semimaru*. The play's setting is the Osaka Barrier, an old toll station on Osaka Pass, between Kyoto and Lake Biwa. All travelers to and from the eastern provinces had to pass this way; the spot became popular in poetry and tales of ordinary life. Among the beggar-entertainers who frequented the Osaka Barrier, one line of blind, roaming musicians claimed Semimaru as a founder and patron. As these blind *biwa* singers sang their alluringly lyrical tales throughout Japan, they not only provided access to a common national story but also helped establish the national language.

Later, these musicians elevated Semimaru into a prince. Whether actual or mythic, Semimaru eventually became a godlike figure to many musicians, especially blind performers. He was honored in a shrine near the Osaka Barrier.

I came to Kyoto to immerse myself in Japanese gardens. I leave with a better understanding not only of the gardens but also about *mono no aware*, which has helped give me a rudimentary understanding of Noh. How might this seemingly intangible idea relate to disability?

I also have added to my miniscule pantheon of Japanese disabled icons: Ebisu, Hōïchi, and now Semimaru.

If the rock garden at Ryoanji taught me experience is not all at once but cumulative, I am still waiting for the revelation that the upper garden at Shugakuin Rikyu promises.

On my way back to Tokyo, I decide to take a slight detour. Three Semimaru shrines remain on the Lake Biwa side of the pass. The largest shrine still boasts the famous "toll station spring" mentioned in the Noh play. The Keihan Electric Railway passes the shrine, covering the shrine's *torii* with rust.

Six

Physical Facts

In 1895 Lafcadio Hearn was appointed to the prestigious position of Chair of English Literature at Tokyo Imperial University, now the University of Tokyo. At the time, the offer of the position puzzled him as he was not an expert: he had no training or degree in English literature, and Japan—flush from victory in the Sino-Japanese War and resentful of the terms imposed by Western powers who feared a powerful Japan and wanted China for themselves—was sending its foreign teachers home.

Hearn soon realized the reason for his hiring. His *Glimpses of Unfamiliar Japan*, published in Boston in 1894, was a huge success. The book revived interest in Japan at a time when American fascination with the country was waning. He was the most prestigious Western writer to fall in love with Japan. His Japanese patrons trusted Hearn to continue to write in praise of the country.

Hearn wrote to a friend, "I fear—I suspect that this position has been given unto me for a combination of reasons, among which the dominant is that I may write at ease many books about Japan."

I want to know more about the blind *biwa* singers of Edo-period Japan. I e-mail a composer friend who lived in Japan a decade ago. He suggests I contact Mika Kimula, a singer he knows and admires. "She knows a lot of artists in Tokyo," my friend writes.

In a polite e-mail exchange, Mika invites me to her concert at a Nippori "live house." Brenda accompanies me to the typically narrow Tokyo building. Going up in the elevator, I notice there is a restaurant on one floor, an office on another, and a hairdresser's salon on another.

On the fourth floor, I claim our tickets at a portable card table at the room's entrance. Just past the ticket table there is a pass-through window from what seems to be a kitchen. The counter of the window serves as a makeshift bar. Everything in the small room is informal.

I look at the single-sheeted typed program. One side is in English; the other in Japanese. The order of songs, all sung in Japanese, will move from the earliest to the most contemporary.

Soon, the room fills up. Brenda and I are the only *gaijin*. Everyone else mills about greeting each other; it seems most of the audience knows each other. Perhaps they are singers and musicians? I wish I could understand what people are saying. The noise of the crowded room gets louder with anticipation.

Lights are flicked off and on. People start taking their seats. Brenda and I sit toward the back of two dozen rows of folding chairs.

A lone man enters the stage. He wears a billowy-sleeved shirt and *hakama* similar to what the Noh musicians in Kyoto wore. He carries a *shakuhachi*, the traditional Japanese flute, a long, reedless instrument made of pale-yellow bamboo.

The first note is low and long, like the sound I made as a child blowing into empty ginger ale bottles—a combination of a foghorn, a human bellow, and the wind.

The next notes are more staccato. As the music continues, it develops into a delicate balance between melody and rhythm. What I am hearing mimics a rushing stream.

When the *shakuhachi* prelude ends, it still reverberates.

Mika Kimula comes onstage. She is dressed in a low-cut, dark-lavender dress. Her hair flows in a long braid down her back. She bows to the *shakuhachi* player, and then—

Mika's voice: neither soprano nor contralto, or both soprano and contralto. Neither Japanese nor Western, or both Japanese and Western. Her low chest notes resonate like a cello. Her high notes are a tremulous, almost Callas-like, vibrato—sometimes clear, sometimes a bit nasal. But the voice is not Maria Callas, nor is it Kathleen Ferrier or Janet Baker or Elisabeth Schwarzkopf or Billie Holiday or Abbey Lincoln or Sarah Vaughan. Mika's voice is like and yet unlike all the singers Ian and I listened to over and over again. One note is beautiful, the next too piercing. Sometimes a note is produced clearly; others sound opaque. She is a singer who is not afraid to make any sound that the music requires, even if it means she might not sound attractive. Each note sounds as if it is the precise expression for the Japanese words she is singing. Of course, I have no idea what the words actually mean.

As the concert progresses, it sounds as if Mika might not be singing words; she could be singing notes—part jazz scat, part onomatopoeia. Hand and facial gestures add depth to notes already filled with a meaning I feel more than I understand. When Mika grabs what seems to be a tambourine and sings "Shite-tan," a contemporary song written for medieval Japanese lyrics, her breath control allows her to sing faster and faster and my heartbeat tries to keep up with her.

The concert ends. During the always-polite Japanese applause, I turn to Brenda. She says, "You're crying."

I make my way to see Mika. I shake her hand. She beams her smile at me, slightly bowing her head.

A few days later, I meet Mika for lunch in Kinshichō, her *shitamachi* neighborhood.

Arriving early, I select a table with a view of the entrance. The moment she walks into the room in a large brimmed blue straw hat and a fitted turquoise one-piece dress, all eyes are on her. Greeting her, I feel as if I am meeting a Japanese version of Sally Bowles. But unlike Christopher Isherwood's creation, Mika has talent.

We sit across from each other, plates of sushi in between. I ask Mika what she knows about the roaming blind *biwa* singers.

"There is still one left! He was part of a recording I did preserving different types of ancient Japanese music. He goes from community to community in Kyūshū, the southern island. Every five years he gives a concert in Tokyo."

"I wonder if Hearn ever heard a *biwa hōshi* when he lived on Kyūshū."

"Ah, so you've been reading Hearn!"

After lunch, I give Mika my three short poems.

I am surprised when she asks, "Have you thought of them as songs?"

"Songs?"

"I have an idea of a composer we can ask to set the poems for Japanese instruments."

"You want to sing my poems?"

"If I am able. I've been singing less since I began having problems with my mouth and jaw, but I should be okay for a concert of your songs while you're in Tokyo."

"Aren't they too 'Orientalist'?"

"Orientalist? What do you mean?"

"I mean I'm a Westerner and I'm writing these short imagistic poems of Japanese gardens. It's almost like Richard Rodgers's 'March of the Siamese Children' in *The King and I*, or Puccini's fake Chinese-isms in *Turandot*." I refrain from mentioning *Madama Butterfly*.

But Mika doesn't. She mentions that to support herself when she was at the fine arts university in Tokyo, she sang in a Ginza nightclub at night. "It was when Ginza was trying to do something different from Roppongi. The nightclub in Ginza asked if I would sing arias from *Madama Butterfly*, accompanied by an electric piano. That's what they thought would attract an upper clientele."

Mika smiles, as do her eyes. She laughs. "Your poems are not Orientalist at all. Your understanding makes me see my culture in an entirely different way. Your excitement for what you see here is catching."

In mid-July, Masa calls me. He is back from Boston. We meet at the waffle restaurant.

"Do your parents know about your boyfriend?" I ask a surrogate question for whether his parents know he is gay.

"They know I have a good friend in Boston. My father doesn't know. My mother, who has met Stuart, knows but she doesn't say anything about it."

"Will you tell Stuart about me?"

"I already told him I met an American writer. And about your physical fact."

Physical fact. What a great phrase to use instead of *disability*. I recognize the irony that this phrase has been given to me by a nonnative English speaker.

After waffles, we go to GB. Masa gets very drunk. As the night progresses, he is slurring his speech to the point where I can't understand what he's saying.

After the bars close, we walk in the pouring rain, searching for a taxi. Emerging from the narrow Nichōme streets, we approach a place where taxis sometimes wait for those leaving the bars. As we are about to get into the taxi together, I make the decision not to spend the night with Masa.

Many years ago, I was involved with an alcoholic, an experience I do not want to repeat.

"I'll talk to you tomorrow," I tell Masa as I settle him in the back seat.

Alone in a taxi on my way home, I think how, years ago, I spent many nights such as this with Miguel, and though the sex was good even when he was drunk, it wasn't worth it.

I make another decision: I will see Masa during the day when, most of the time, he has not yet started to drink.

Back at my apartment, I hear the ticking clock.

In Japan, I find myself calculating the time difference between where I am and the northeastern U.S., where most of my friends, especially Ian, live. If I call Ian now, it will be morning in DC. Perhaps I can catch him on his way to work. The call goes to voice mail.

When we first separated, Ian talked about visiting me in Japan. But since I have arrived, he does not respond to my question about whether he will do so. Instead, he tells me he is wary of what he calls my "romanticization" of Japan. When I share my experiences of this still-unfamiliar culture I am just beginning to understand, he wants explanations for things I can't explain.

During my time in Japan, I have gotten used to looking at things differently. More and more, I accept what I find in front of me. Whereas in the States, I quickly formed and spoke of my opinions about what I saw and the people I met, in Tokyo, although not indiscriminate, I have suspended such judgments, befriending many I would never have befriended in the U.S. Since the Japanese I meet don't psychologize—why did this person do that? why does this person like that person?—I don't ask these questions.

Like the Japanese, I decide to understand his nonanswer as no. Ian will not be coming to visit me in Japan.

I'm having coffee with Rafael, the Venezuelan expat I met at GB. After seven years of living in Japan, he is thinking of leaving.

"Why leave Japan?" I ask, not knowing that months later I would be asked—and be asking—this same question.

"I'm tired of being treated as different all the time because I'm a *gaijin*."

What Rafael says stays with me. I know there is nowhere I can go where I feel I fit in entirely. But here, being a *gaijin* comes first, not being disabled. In Japan I am treated as a foreigner because I am a foreigner, an outsider, while in the United States, my native country, I am treated as an outsider when I'm not. So far, in Japan my disability has been treated routinely as nothing more or less than a physical fact.

I also know that here I am shielded from expectation by being a *gaijin*. I am treated well because I am a writer visiting on a prestigious grant. Not understanding the language—I can't even read a Japanese menu to order my food in a restaurant—I have to trust those who guide me.

As I open the door to my apartment, the phone is ringing. It is Brenda. I am surprised to hear from her. This weekend, her last before she leaves Japan, she is supposed to be away with Taka at a friend's house near the ocean. But she is home and wants to come downstairs.

"We spent Friday night and Saturday holed up together in the ocean house," she tells me, catching her breath from rushing down the stairs. "Then, early on Saturday night, an older couple arrived. The three of them, the older couple and Taka, talked furiously in Japanese, which I couldn't much follow. Finally, Taka turned to me and introduced the woman as his mother."

"His mother? Was the guy with her his father?"

"I thought it was his father, too. But when I went out to smoke and Taka followed me outside, he told me it was his mother's boyfriend."

"Her boyfriend?"

"Yes. Her boyfriend."

"Did his father know?"

"I'm sure he *knew*, but I'm not sure he *knew*. This is Japan."

"Didn't Taka tell his mother he was going to be at the house?"

"I guess not. But get this, what all that Japanese argument was about wasn't that Taka was with me at the same time as his mother and her boyfriend. His mother was upset that she only had brought food for two!"

Brenda and I can't stop laughing.

"It was all too weird. I needed another cigarette. Taka took the hint and again followed me outside. I told him I couldn't stay in the house with his mother, that I needed to go back to Tokyo. I don't know what he told them, probably that I wasn't feeling well or something. We drove back to Tokyo tonight."

In a few days, Brenda will be gone. Tokyo won't be the same without her.

Seven

A Mountain of Skulls and Candlelit Graves

In Lafcadio Hearn's tale "The Mountain of Skulls," a bodhisattva guides a pilgrim up a steep mountain where "neither token of water, nor trace of plant, nor shadow of flying bird" can be found. The two climbers climb higher; the pilgrim looks down: "For there was not any ground,—neither beneath him nor about him nor above him,—but a heaping only, monstrous and measureless, of skull and fragments of skulls and dust of bone."

The pilgrim is horrified. "I fear!—unutterably I fear! . . . there is nothing but the skulls of men!"

"A mountain of skulls it is," says the bodhisattva. "But know, my son, that all of them are your own! Each has at some time been the nest of your dreams and delusions and desires. Not even one of them is the skull of any other being. All,—all without exception,—have been yours, in the billions of your former lives."

It probably takes ten minutes—but it is as if time has stopped—for me to realize there is a woman rising from the floor of the dark stage.

At first, the only sound I hear might be the hiss-static of speakers playing nothing with the volume turned too loud. Slowly, I discern the familiar strains of "Amazing Grace," played by an unfamiliar wind instrument.

Even more slowly, I see the butoh dancer I have come to see: Mikami Kayo, her face and body painted Kabuki-white, covered by tree branches—or is she wearing the branches? it is still too dark to tell— begins to move. At first a toe. Then a finger. Then a leg. A hand. Until it seems as if her back is arched fully backward. Each part of her body, including eyes and mouth, seems to move independently. I cannot tell what is hand, what is foot, what is face, or what is backside.

Finally, gravity is defeated: the woman is standing.

As the music plays, increasingly louder and louder, she begins to sway, moving sideways, forward, and backward, all seemingly at the same time. She has complete control of every digit of every limb. Watching what I think is a primordial ritual, I feel as if I, too, have slowly been brought to my feet. I check with my hands; I am still seated.

The music stops. A group of multisized women darts to the front of the stage and stares at the audience—like the Harajuku girls in their white face paint. I can clearly see the red on the insides of mouths, at the edges of eyes.

The music changes to something akin to French cabaret. Four tall men, their height emphasized by the large Victorian dresses they wear, overtake the stage. This group of tall men and this group of multisized women and Mikami Kayo cross paths during many scenes, each ending in a blackout and a change of music, until, once again, Mikami Kayo, the woman who started the performance, descends, slow movement by slow movement, back into the ground.

After the performance, I roam the theater lobby, where the performers are serving and drinking beer. I approach Mikami-san, who seems so much smaller offstage than on, though her round face contains the same intensity of her performance.

I hold both of Mikami-san's hands in mine, give her my *meishi*, and gesture to ask if I can take her picture. Mikami-san graciously puts her arm around my shoulder. I hug her warmly and although I have no idea if she knows what I am saying, I tell her I cannot wait to see her perform again.

On the subway back to Meijirodai, I begin to think of butoh as contemporary Japan's expression of *mono no aware*, "the beauty of temporal things." It was like watching the entire life process, from birth to death, but I couldn't tell which was which. Was Mikami-san learning to walk or learning to die?

Obon is the mid-August Japanese festival celebrating ancestors. During Obon most Japanese return to their familial residence. Families decorate their houses with lanterns to help guide the ancestral spirits home.

Not having a family in Japan, I don't know what to do for Obon. MM suggests I go to Kōyasan for the famous Obon Festival.

Kūkai, better known as Kōbō Daishi, introduced Shingon Buddhism to Japan in 805 AD, after returning from a boat trip to China. Kōbō Daishi is enshrined in eternal meditation at Okunoin cemetery on Kōyasan. The night before Obon, thousands of worshippers light a two-kilometer path through Okunoin leading to the Torodo, Kōbō Daishi's burial chamber guarded by a thousand lamps, two of which are believed to have been continuously lit for nine hundred years.

I arrive on Kōyasan in the afternoon. I am relieved that among the tall cedar trees on the top of the mountain, it is much cooler than the brutal humid heat of the Japanese summer. There are no hotels on Kōyasan. The only lodgings on the forested mountaintop are in *shukubo*, simple temple lodgings in tatami-matted rooms. Guests are served *shojin ryori*, vegetarian meals eaten by monks, and are welcome at the daily six o'clock morning prayers.

After leaving my things at the *shukubo*, I decide to see Okunoin while it is still daylight. This afternoon I am the only visitor on the paths along the Tamagawa. The leaves rustle in the breeze at the top of the trees; shadows fall on the over two hundred thousand tombs.

Before I came to Japan, I knew of the Buddhist belief in cremation. But I didn't know that Buddhist temple grounds included cemeteries. After cremation, what is the use of a grave? I didn't know that Buddhist graves inter the ashes of the dead.

Okunoin is the largest cemetery in Japan. It is also spooky. The old section contains large *nishinoya*, stone lanterns, most with a yin-yang symbol with an open crescent incised in the stone to emit light. These *nishinoya* line the paths leading through gravesites of former feudal lords.

The tombs are composed of weathered lichen-stained fallen stones and large wooden poles dampened by the forest humidity. Often, indecipherable kanji are incised in the stones and poles. I pass some tombs that look like small houses guarded by stone-slatted fences. Some have *torii*-gated entrances, showing how, over the years, Buddhism has absorbed Shinto beliefs.

Other tombs are stupa-shaped, angular stones on top of round stones on top of rectangular stones; others have representational statues of Kannon, pilgrims in pointed straw hats, and countless smaller statues of *jizu*, the deity who protects children and is often seen at a child's grave.

In the cemetery's newer section are company-owned tombs. Here, Japanese kitsch even reaches the dead: United Coffee Company's tomb has a large marble coffee cup; another has a towering metal rocket. I search for the White Ant Monument, supposedly donated by a pesticide company to atone for the suffering caused to the insects its products killed, but I can't find it.

The path gently rises as I get closer to the Torodo, the hall of lamps, which guards Kōbō Daishi's grave. I pass huge stupa-shaped tombs that look like mini-pyramids. Getting closer to these mounds, I notice they are made up of countless niches, and in the niches are countless *jizu*, each eerily adorned with offerings of childlike garb—bibs, hats, scarves, even pajamas emblazoned with familiar anime characters, including Pikachu, my totem yellow Pokémon.

I decide to turn back before crossing the river, leaving the sacred visit to Kōbō Daishi's grave for this evening's Obon procession.

After dinner, I walk back to Okunoin. As I approach the cemetery, the streets become increasingly crowded. Looking back from where we came, I see orange-robed monks carrying a huge, flaming tree. When the monks reach the cemetery entrance, they stop so other monks can light candles from the tree's flame.

The crowd follows the monks, so I follow, too. The orderly procession continues on the cemetery paths; small children run alongside us distributing candles. Since my afternoon visit, the paths have been lined with aluminum foil. Sticks protrude from the foil. A few lit candles are atop some sticks. People from the procession begin to stop. They light their candles from the already lit ones and leave them on the empty sticks. In this way, those in front light the path for those who follow.

Soon, as the path moves further into the forest, the evening darkens. The flickering flames from the candles are the only light on the path to Kōbō Daishi's grave.

Every so often, I replenish my supply of candles at small tables set up on the side of the path. Stopping at a table, I look back down the sloping path now lit by thousands of candles.

I stop again before crossing over the river to Kōbō Daishi's grave. In the middle of the river are large upright planks in remembrance of children who have drowned. At the river crossing are five large *jizu* statues of darkened stone. The custom is to douse the statues with water from the purification fountains at the base of each statue before crossing the river.

I take the large bamboo ladle. I wash, in turn, each *jizu*. My dead— even those I have not remembered for many years—gather around me: my boyfriend Alex, my acupuncturist Paul, the poets Tede Matthews and Melvin Dixon, all dead of AIDS; the actress Kathy Leavelle, my former boss and San Francisco friend, dead from lung cancer; my parents' friend Civia's son, Larry, her daughter, Nancy, her infant granddaughter, Larry's wife, Cindy, dead from a car accident when hit by a drunk driver outside Civia's Florida home. With each ladle of water, each dousing of a *jizu*, more of my dead return to accompany me to Kōbō Daishi's grave across the river.

A thousand eternally lit bronze lamps surround the Torodo. The long procession lines up to pass around the gates—always closed— guarding the cave in which Kōbō Daishi sits, where he is said to have rested in eternal meditation for over a thousand years.

It is believed that when Kōbō Daishi is ready for Buddhahood, he will take all those enshrined on Kōyasan with him. In the meantime, he awaits the arrival of Maitreya, the bodhisattva who will become the Future Buddha who will save all those unable to achieve enlightenment.

I wonder if anyone has ever entered the cave. If they did enter, what would they find?

I follow the path around the mausoleum and pass the building that holds additional lamps and scriptures before recrossing the river, leaving my dead behind to wait with Kōbō Daishi.

Back on the other side of the river, I don't want to walk through the candlelit cemetery again. I remember Allan's story of his first visit to a Japanese cemetery. Leaving the cemetery, Yoshihiro asked if he saw the *bakemono* on his shoulder.

Leaving the cemetery, I look back across the river to the Torodo.

I can no longer see my dead. But I feel as if I am somehow more complete, more integrated, as if my past finally has caught up with the present.

On my walk back to the *shukubo*, I don't know how to explain what happened when I doused the *jizu* statues with water. Is this why I came to Japan? To ferry my dead across the Tamagawa? I think about what the bodhisattva in Hearn's "A Mountain of Skulls" says about the skulls: *All, — all without exception — have been yours, in the billions of your former lives.*

And I realize that the dead I saw were dead too young, too early. If, according to Buddhism, they were taken from this life because of something their ancestors did, I don't know what those actions might be. If I were to believe this, I would have to believe that there was a reason I was disabled, something I gave up thinking a very long time ago.

When I return to the *shukubo*, on the futon in my temple lodgings, I am kept awake by the candlelight still flickering before my eyes.

I remember what the priest tells Hōïchi: *All that you have been imagining was illusion — except the calling of the dead.*

My last thought before sleep is of Ian, surely someone I do not count among my dead. But he is the only person I know who is familiar with all the dead who had returned to me earlier in the night. The only person who could understand what I experienced is halfway around the world, where his day has just begun.

The next morning I awake at 5:30 a.m. and make my way to the temple prayer hall. I sit silently listening to the rhythmic chanting of the monks, remembering how I fell asleep when Alex and I meditated together when we lived in our Victorian house on Carl Street in San Francisco.

This morning, on Kōyasan, though my eyes are closed, I do not fall asleep. I am startled by what comes into my mind: last night, did I think of Ian because, in a way, he was taken from me before I thought it was time?

At the end of the prayer session, I rise and walk to the altar, where I leave an offering of coins and a stick of burning incense.

Before descending Kōyasan, I buy a drawing of Kōbō Daishi, which I send to Ian when I return to Tokyo.

Eight

||||||||

An Infected Throat and a Healing Tree

I begin to link butoh's fascination with the grotesque to Western movements such as Surrealism and Absurdism. Despite these connections, butoh remains to me a distinctly Japanese form. And as it matured, its avant-garde, antitradition pedigree begins to reveal its links to other traditional Japanese art forms such as Noh.

And despite butoh founder Hijikata's protest to the contrary, the landscape of butoh cannot in my mind be separated from Japan's experience of the aftermath of the atomic bombings of Hiroshima and Nagasaki. Perhaps Donald Richie says it best: "Here is a postwar wasteland whose . . . inhabitants held aloft pathetic emblems of a vanished civilization. . . . Hijikata's picture was not the end of the world but, specifically, the end of Japan."

What else can explain Waguri Yukio's performance, during which he digs into a mound of dirt at the front of the stage, discovering what seems to be a corpse? Holding the corpse in his arms, he slowly but ecstatically dances to John Lennon's "Love Is Real," all the time looking not at the corpse he holds but up at the sky.

The black curtain at the back of the stage opens to reveal a small shrine-like box decorated with Christmas lights. As the music gets louder and louder, the dancer approaches the makeshift shrine, and it is as if he has unearthed his own body: he is communing with his sacrificed self, consumed with all the joy and all the decay that his body experienced while alive.

I want to talk with disabled *hibakusha*, literally bomb-affected people. The *hibakusha* might help me better understand how the Japanese view the disabled. Are the lives of the *hibakusha* similar to other disabled Japanese?

In August I e-mail Rahna Reiko Rizzuto, a writer who last year spent her fellowship in Hiroshima. She suggests I contact the World Friendship Center. The center sets up a mid-September interview with Numata-san, a well-known *hibakusha* who lost her right leg on August 6, 1945. I decide to be in Hiroshima when my parents will be visiting Japan for my father's seventieth birthday. I want to experience firsthand my parents' reaction to Hiroshima's Peace Memorial Museum, to see how they react to the "other" part of the war. As Jews, they habitually view the war through the prism of the Holocaust.

But I almost don't make it to Hiroshima. My original plans do not work out the way I had hoped. It is a very hot and humid summer, even by Tokyo standards. Never before have I been in a place where after the rain, the humidity increases. The summer heat, combined with my extremely active life in and out of Tokyo, has taken its toll. I have lost over twenty pounds since arriving in Japan.

Three days before my parents' arrival, I am at the Hakone Open Air Museum to see an installation inspired by the Japanese teahouse. I tour the outdoor museum in the sweltering heat, sweating even more profusely than usual. I think this is due to the strong midday sun. Back at my hotel, I eat dinner and go to sleep.

When I wake the next morning, I can barely lift my head from the pillow. I get myself to the bathroom and start vomiting. Heat stroke, I figure. Somehow, I'm able to pack up and make my way to the station. I endure the hour-and-a-half train ride back to Tokyo. I take a taxi back to my apartment.

I find the Fahrenheit thermometer I have brought with me and take my temperature: 103°. I immediately call Eiko-san, my landlady, whose husband is a doctor affiliated with a hospital not too far away. She calls the hospital and arranges for me to be seen in the morning. But how will I make it until then?

I call Masa. He comes over and, although he is drunk by midnight, cooks a homemade chicken soup. He feeds me tiny spoonfuls as he sits on the side of the bed.

In the morning Eiko-san and Masa take me to the hospital. My fever has spiked over 104°. I pass out before I am taken to what will be my room. My blood is drawn to determine what is going on. My throat is so sore I can't swallow.

The patient, the sickness may last long, but is sure to get well.

"How long will I be here?" I ask the young female Japanese doctor as Masa interprets. "My parents will be here from the United States on Friday."

"You will be here for a while, probably a week, depending on how long it takes for us to know what is the cause," the doctor tells me. "Your fever remains high and you are severely dehydrated. It seems you have a serious infection in your throat."

It is already Wednesday afternoon, which is Tuesday night in New York. I know my parents will be leaving their upstate house in the morning to get to the airport in New York City. I won't be able to meet them when they get here. I give Masa their phone number so he can call to tell them I am okay but sick with a throat infection in the hospital. I will have to arrange for someone to meet them at their hotel when they arrive in Tokyo on Friday night.

The doctor asks my medical history. "Medications?"

"Paxil, an antidepressant."

"Why?"

"Depression and anxiety."

"With a psychiatrist?"

"For twenty years." I notice the doctor raise a questioning eyebrow when Masa translates this to her. I do not think she has ever heard of, or even contemplated, someone seeing a psychiatrist for a year, let alone for as long as I'd been in therapy.

On Thursday MM comes to the hospital. He brings me flowers. "Bought from my daughter the florist. I never bought flowers from her before." MM smiles his wide smile.

Eiko-san visits when MM is still in my room. She bows deeply to him and looks at me. "How do you know such a famous man to my generation? You have such a wonderful time in Japan," she says before bowing to MM once again. "Everyone is good to you."

"I will meet your parents at their hotel on Friday night," MM tells me. "I will bring them to see you here."

By Friday my fever has abated but the infection remains. That night my parents arrive in Tokyo. MM meets them at their hotel and escorts them to the hospital. Masa, Allan, and Mika are with me when they arrive.

My father's main concern during most of my childhood and young adult life was my well-being. He sees my friends surrounding me in my hospital bed. He relaxes and holds my hand.

"Not what I had planned for your arrival," I say. "I'm glad you'll have the chance to see Japan."

Two days later it is my father's birthday. Although I am still on IV, my fever is almost normal and the infection is finally starting to get better. I had arranged a special dinner at a small restaurant in Ginza. I do not want to miss the dinner.

"My father's seventieth birthday is today," I inform the doctor. "We have a special dinner in Ginza."

"You can go," the doctor proclaims. "We will detach your IV. I order you to go."

That night I am still weak and very dizzy. But the doctor patches up my arm; I will once again have the IV connected when I return to the hospital later that night. Masa pushes me in a wheelchair to the hospital exit.

MM meets us in Ginza. At the small Ginza restaurant, designed to look like a traditional rustic Japanese country home, we are served the preordered eight-course "Yuki" dinner. I sit with my back braced against a wall and enjoy watching my mother eat what is to her "strange food."

"What's this?" she keeps asking Masa, who patiently explains what each course is. He makes sure that my mother, who does not want to eat raw fish, is not served sushi or sashimi.

A waitress carries a cake with lit candles to our table. Somehow, someone had told the restaurant to have a cake for my father's seventieth birthday. My father is surprised, and as he blows out his birthday candles, he begins to cry.

Late at night, I am once again alone in my hospital bed. I am exhausted. But I'm glad I had the chance to see my parents experience some of the hospitality and care I have received during my time in Japan. They saw how I have managed, in a matter of months, to build a life for myself halfway around the world.

And I have managed, with the help of my friends, a medical crisis, in a place so different from what I'm used to back home. Could it be my disability experience that has allowed me to navigate a culture where I don't know what most people are saying or most of the signs are telling me? Has being disabled, where change is the norm, taught me to find my way through difference? After all, being disabled since birth, I've grown up and become accustomed to living in a culture different from my own.

Two days later my parents are on their way to Kyoto. Masa accompanies me from the hospital in a taxi to my apartment.

For two weeks I barely have the strength to go out. I have to discontinue the antibiotic that, when changed from IV to pill form, causes a rash all over my body. It is already the end of September, and, although

I have extended my stay for a month, I know my time in Japan will soon be coming to an end. Less than a week after Mika's concert of the garden songs in November, I will be leaving Japan.

For the concert I have finished six of what I think will be a sequence of eight or nine poems. The composer only has time to write the music for two. Just as well, since Mika, still bothered by her jaw, can focus more closely on the two songs she will sing. The evening will be a combination of the songs, my reading of the poems, and my giving a talk about how I came to write the poems in Japan.

Most of all I want to interview Numata-san in Hiroshima. My stay in Japan will not seem complete without meeting at least one disabled *hibakusha*.

So far, my research about disability in Japan has been scattered, incomplete; no big picture has yet emerged. For every successful Fukushima-sensei, there seems to be a frustrated person denied a job because of their disability. I have uncovered hints of a rich disability history in the culture of the blind *biwa hōshi* but have yet to locate the supposedly disabled Ebisu in the complicated pantheon of Japanese gods.

In Japan for close to six months, I am still treated as any other *gaijin*, not as the disabled person I am treated as back in my own country. I am still more comfortable informing those I meet in Japan about disability in the U.S. than talking about what I have found here in Japan.

The World Friendship Center is able to reschedule my interview with Numata-san, although with a different translator. Despite still feeling far from 100 percent, I decide to go ahead with my trip to Hiroshima.

For some reason, I have imagined Hiroshima to be like Ferrara, the Ferrara I first knew from De Sica's movie version of *The Garden of the Finzi-Continis*. I imagined bicyclists peddling along wide, ghostly boulevards; survivors still affected by wartime events out of their control;

and the air still filled with scars of radiation even though the bomb had been dropped over fifty-seven years ago.

I arrive in Hiroshima the afternoon before I am scheduled to interview Numata-san. By the time I check into my hotel, it is too late to go to the Peace Memorial Museum. I take the streetcar to the north side of Peace Park. I walk across the reconstructed T-shaped Aioi Bridge, the target for the bomb. The bomb actually exploded only three hundred meters southeast of its target, quite accurate since this was done without radar, using only the naked eye, approximately 580 meters above the Shima Hospital in a busy downtown Hiroshima district then known as Saiku-machi.

On the banks of the Motayasu River, I reach the ruined building known as the A-Bomb Dome, 160 meters northwest of where the bomb exploded. The red brick building originally opened in 1915 as the Hiroshima Prefectural Commercial Exhibition Hall. During the war, as Japan's economy declined, the hall was commandeered for government and rationing offices. The building's architectural skeleton and dome somehow survived the blast that killed all its occupants on the morning of August 6, 1945.

In the twilight, I find the Children's Peace Monument, also known as the Tower of the Paper Cranes, a memorial inspired by Sasaki Sadako. Sadako was two at the time of the bombing. She developed leukemia when she was twelve. While in the hospital, Sadako thought that if she could fold a thousand paper cranes, according to Japanese legend, her wish would be granted: she would survive. Sadako had reached 644 paper cranes when she died on October 25, 1955.

Sadako's fellow students finished folding the cranes. They were instrumental in building this monument to their dead classmate and the thousands of children who died from the bombing. Streams of multicolored paper cranes, looking like phosphorescent psychedelic wigs from the 1960s, are left at Sadako's memorial, as well as at the other places of remembrance throughout Peace Park. The bell in the center of the monument is in the shape of a gold paper crane.

I ring the bell. The echo through the empty park scares some birds that quickly fly away.

I make my way to the Cenotaph, the central monument to those killed by the A-bomb. The Cenotaph is in a shape evoking primitive shelters of the Kofun Period (300 to 600 AD); its parabolic arch is reminiscent of *haniwa*, the pottery found in prehistoric Japanese tombs, representing what the deceased might find useful in the afterlife.

Walking in the hauntingly quiet park, I try to imagine this island in the middle of two rivers as Hiroshima's once-bustling Saiku-machi district.

The next day I interview Numata-san at the International Conference Center, just west of the Peace Memorial Museum. Mariko serves as translator. I hope not only to hear Numata-san's *hibakusha* story but also to learn how her disability influenced her life after the war.

"I was a military girl," Numata-san begins. "I believed Japan would win the war and I would do anything for Japan to win the war." She shows me a map of the city, familiar from my walk in the park yesterday afternoon. On the map the hypocenter is circled. Also circled is the school, converted to wartime use, where Numata-san was working at 8:15 a.m. on August 6, 1945, when the A-bomb exploded. The night before, sirens warned that B-29 bombers might be approaching, but by morning the all-clear signal had sounded; it was once again safe to go out into the streets.

"We always wondered why no B-29-san hit Hiroshima," she tells me. "We kept waiting for that to happen."

When the building collapsed, a beam fell on top of her. "I must have passed out, I don't remember. The next thing I knew I heard my mother's voice. She had come looking for me and found someone to help her move the building beam off of her daughter. That's how I lost my leg. For many years I taught in school. After I retired, a few years ago, I finally realized I was disabled and found a group for older disabled women. Only with them did I find I could once again complain."

Even though I specifically wanted to talk to a disabled *hibakusha*, this is the only time Numata-san mentions being disabled. It is as if the experience of the A-bomb, of being a *hibakusha*, subsumes all her identity, leaving little room for being, more commonly, disabled.

Numata-san's story of what happened on August 6, 1945, and the following days does not differ from the other stories I have read in preparation for my trip to Hiroshima. But about a year after the bomb was dropped, something happened to Numata-san.

"I had given up hope," Numata-san confesses. "Then one day I was by the river and I saw this tree—I will take you to see it after lunch; I would like to take you to lunch after we've finished here—and I noticed this tree had died in the bomb blast. It was still black and charred, but I noticed small branches beginning to grow. Somehow the tree had found a way to come back to life. And I thought, if this tree can do it, so can I. I came to visit the tree many times. When they built Peace Park, they moved the tree so it was easier for everyone to see."

I accompany Numata-san and Mariko to the small café off the lobby of the museum. Numata-san points out the window. "That is the tree. We will visit it after lunch."

During lunch many people stop to say hello to Numata-san and Mariko. Mariko talks to a woman who has approached our table. The woman turns to me and says, "You are Kenny-san. How amazing! I'm Keiko. I was supposed to be your interpreter but you were sick in September. We had been in touch by e-mail. I am so glad you have been able to come to Hiroshima."

Keiko-san joins us for the remainder of our lunch. When she accompanies us outside to see the tree, I notice that she limps. Like me, one of her legs is shorter than the other.

"Have you seen the museum?" she asks.

"Not yet. I was going to go this afternoon."

"Let me be your guide."

After lunch we take photos under Numata-san's thin-branched tree. Without Numata-san's story, the tree would just be an ordinary tree. Is this the actual tree that Numata-san had seen on the riverbank, the tree that inspired her to survive? I think about the myth my parents have told for decades about my childhood—how although I was never supposed to walk, I learned to walk in two casts—and I feel closer to Numata-san than I did while listening to her story. I understand the need for the tree planted by the museum to be Numata-san's tree.

I give Numata-san and Mariko *omiyage*, traditional thank-you gifts. We bow and bow and continue bowing until we finally part.

I follow Keiko-san into the museum. She narrates the history of Hiroshima, which led to its being a target for the bomb. By 1895, during the Sino-Japanese War, the Imperial Headquarters, Japan's supreme military command, was moved to Hiroshima. Hiroshima became the embarkation point for army troops going overseas. More and more military facilities were built. *I was a military girl.*

The by-now-familiar story is retold: The clear, cloudless Monday morning. The mobilization to make fire lanes in the city. The mobilized middle school students working at factories; the evacuation of third graders to the countryside. The previous night's air-raid warning at 12:25 a.m.; the all clear at 2:10 a.m.; another alert at 7:09 a.m., lifted at 7:31 a.m. The "irony" of Hiroshima not being the target of a previous air raid, now "explained" by the United States wanting to know the effects of an atomic bomb on an undisturbed city. The cost of the bomb, one of the reasons for dropping it: all that money had to be put to some use. The explosion of the bomb at 8:15 a.m. The mushroom cloud.

The second part of the museum is filled with the effects of the bomb: The burned lunchbox once belonging to a mobilized student who worked six hundred meters from the hypocenter. A human shadow burned into the stone stairs of a bank. A white wall stained with black rain, which contained large amounts of radioactive soot and dust, contaminating areas far from the hypocenter. The charred skeleton of a child's tricycle. The cracked face of a pocket watch stopped at 8:15 a.m.

In the section devoted to birth defects due to radiation, I become self-conscious, like I did at the Holocaust Museum in Washington, DC, when I reached the section on the Nazi extermination of the disabled. I cannot process the numerous facts on how radiation affects the body's cells. I think about how much radiation I have been exposed to via X-rays. I wonder about Keiko-san's limp.

"I must make an appointment," Keiko-san says as we leave the final exhibit.

"Thank you so much for this afternoon. I am so glad we had the chance to meet. Such a coincidence."

"Peace activists all know each other in Hiroshima," she tells me as I bow my good-bye.

In the museum store, I ask if Numata-san's book is available in English, and I'm not sure the woman behind the counter knows what I'm saying. I do not find Numata-san's book; I buy other books instead, as well as postcards.

It is almost twilight when I once again find myself in Peace Park. I make my way to the streetcar that will take me back to my hotel. I once again stop in front of the A-Bomb Dome. After my day in Hiroshima, I now think of the ruins as a monument as much to reconstruction as to destruction.

Back at the hotel, I am physically and emotionally drained. I sort through the day's images. Neither the objective numbing numbers (1,000,000° Celsius, 35 percent energy released as heat rays, 50 percent as blast, 15 percent as radiation [5 percent as initial radiation, 10 percent as residual radiation]; of 350,000 in Hiroshima, 140,000 dead) nor new words (hypocenter, cenotaph, keloid) nor old dates (July 16, 1945; August 6, 1945; August 15, 1945) can successfully tell the story of what happened in Japan.

Numata-san's story transforms from that of aggressor to victim, from victim to survivor. Her story is filled with both guilt and innocence, with as much shame as pride. But Numata-san's telling of her story seems fixed, closed. Even the story of her tree, which actually might not be her tree, seems scripted. Even if I had asked more questions, I know that I could not interrupt, or disturb, her story.

How can I find a way to tie together these seemingly incomplete narratives, as moving as they are, not only in Hiroshima but also throughout my stay in Japan? What am I missing? What ties them together remains unseen.

Nine

Borrowing the Hills

In his story "A Conservative," Lafcadio Hearn follows the life of a samurai's son who grows up in the feudal world of the samurai, in a city "where no foreigner had ever been," reaching manhood "in that innocent provincial life of Old Japan," where "a young samurai might grow up exceptionally pure-minded and simple-hearted."

But the arrival of Commodore Perry's black ships changes everything. From a British teacher, he learns English and meets a missionary who introduces him to the New Testament. He converts to Christianity and travels to Europe.

What he finds surprises him: "That world had no faith. It was a world of mockery and masquerade and pleasure-seeking selfishness. . . . Foreign civilization had taught him to understand, as he could never otherwise have understood, the worth and beauty of his own."

Hearn was invited to give a series of lectures in London and in the United States. But he never returned to the West. He died in Tokyo from heart failure on September 30, 1904. He was fifty-four years old.

In Japan I am often asked, "What is it like to be disabled in Japan?"
"I can't answer that question" has become my usual reply. "I'm not Japanese. Each disabled person's impairment is different. I can only tell you about my experience as a disabled *gaijin*, a Westerner, with my specific disability."

But no matter how I reply during my talks, this question keeps following me: *What is it like to be disabled in Japan?*

By the time I've been in Japan for six months, I finally have a story to tell in answer to this question.

At an *onsen*, a hot springs resort, the child-size *yukata* is far too small for me. Even the smallest adult-size *yukata* is too long for my foreshortened legs. No matter how I tie the obi sash of the *yukata*, I trip when walking to and from dinner or to and from the baths. To make matters more complicated, I've never been good at tying things, even my shoes. The *yukata* might open, exposing my naked body to whomever I am dining with or whoever happens to be walking by.

One late October afternoon, at an *onsen* high in the Japan Alps, after leaving the private bath, I rearrange my *yukata* so I won't trip or find myself suddenly naked on my way back to my room. An elderly Japanese woman with two small children—I assume they are her grandchildren—approaches me. Without saying a word—she probably assumes, correctly, I don't understand much Japanese and, even if she is able to speak English, a woman of her generation probably would be too shy to speak English to a naked *gaijin*—she hikes up my *yukata* and shows me how to tie the obi sash so it bunches the *yukata* under it, adapting the *yukata* to the appropriate size for my body.

While doing this, the elderly woman realizes, at the same time that I do, I have accidentally put on the *yukata* inside out. We laugh together.

"*Domo arigato gozaimashita,*" I say over and over, thanking the woman very much as I bow deeply before she returns to her grandchildren.

Making my way back to the room, I do not trip on the *yukata*. It stays in place, fastened tightly under the obi. For me, this is how it feels to be a disabled *gaijin* in Japan.

Why are you leaving Japan?" asks someone in the audience at the November premiere of the first two garden songs.

The easy answer: my grant is over. But technically my grant ended a month ago. I have stayed longer than initially planned.

My money ran out. But I could stay in Japan and still teach in the graduate writing program I have taught in for over a decade. I only have to be on campus for two weeks every year; the rest of the year, I work with my students through the mail. And I now know enough people in Japan. I could probably find some work in Tokyo to supplement my teaching income.

I have to finish writing my Darwin book. This might be more truthful. I am still overstimulated. Besides the garden poems and the talks I have given, I have not written a word about Darwin while in Japan.

I need to find out what my relationship with Ian might be. Somehow it does not yet feel over.

Perhaps, the question to ask is: why would I stay?

My research is filled with dead ends. Too much remains unfinished.

If you have right mind, your request will be granted later on. Six months after receiving this fortune at Sensō-ji, my request for Ian to come to Japan has not been granted. I still do not have the "right mind." I remember how the view in the upper garden at Shugakuin-Rikyu is delayed for maximum impact, until it can be seen as a seamless whole. Somehow, for some reason I do not yet know, I must not yet be ready to see the big picture.

The two weeks before departure are filled with rehearsals for the concert. As the concert approaches, I become more and more nervous.

Over the years, I have never felt nervous before a public appearance. But now it is as if all the emotion of my stay in Japan has risen to the surface and overflows. I know I have to prepare a talk about the poems that have become songs. I know I will have to talk about my other experiences in Japan. But how?

I know that, soon after arriving in Japan, I was overwhelmed with the abundance of new experiences, and I could not understand all I was seeing and feeling. I just had to experience what was before me. I knew I could not ask why.

I know that among these new experiences, two keep recurring: Mika's voice and the irises of Meiji Jingu. I had come to Japan to learn about the lives of disabled Japanese. But as I spent more time in the gardens of Japan, I found myself writing not about disability but about Japanese gardens.

On the surface these poems seem to be about what I saw: the flowers, the teahouses, the rocks, the bridges. But now, at the end of my stay in Japan, I realize that what I was actually writing about was what was held in the gardens: a microcosm of what it means to be alive in an ever-changing mortal world. And living life in a mortal world is perhaps the greatest lesson learned from the experience of living with a disability.

Mono no aware. There is nothing more constant—or moving—than change.

As I told Mika when I first gave her the poems, when I began writing the poems, I was embarrassed they would seem too artificially "Oriental." But Mika's encouragement—*Your understanding makes me see my culture in an entirely different way. Your excitement for what you see and experience here is catching*—kept me going. I soon realized that what I was writing somehow seemed similar to the poems I had written about Alex, my HIV-positive boyfriend, twelve years ago.

The poems I wrote in Japan lead me back to where I began when I started writing poems. Not only in form but in content as well. Just as I wrote of borrowing others' words in an earlier poem, now, in the garden poems, I borrow from the Japanese landscape as well as from ancient Chinese poems. I evoke the Heian period *waka* parties in which contestants sat on the banks of a garden's stream writing short poems before a cup of saké floated by. I have learned to look at life by employing *shakkei*, by borrowing Japan—its history, its art, its culture, all manifested in its gardens—to live my daily life more clearly.

But clarity is not knowing. I keep questioning.

Was Mika right? Could the poems I wrote be songs? And, if so, how could my English words reverberate when accompanied by the sounds of Japanese music? Might the music help a Japanese audience understand my English words? Might these songs be the common space between different cultures that Allan described when telling me about his relationship with Yoshihiro, the space that never truly developed in my relationship with Masa?

The days before the concert, I keep asking: Why am I so comfortable here? Why does Tokyo seem, in so many ways, after such a short time, home?

Once again at night, walking along the Edogawa near my apartment, I think about how before I came to Japan, I wondered what my Tokyo nights would be like, how I would manage on my own. I never watched a DVD on my computer. Since arriving in Japan, I can count on one hand the nights I have spent alone.

Watching the Edogawa very slowly move down its path, I realize in Japan that because my body is dealt with by those I have met as a *physical fact*, the phrase Masa gave to me soon after we met, I have learned to do so, as well.

Yet all of this seems too easy. The reasons I feel at home in Japan are less obvious. Something in Japanese culture accepts me. Somehow, my time in Japan has brought me back to a place I had not been in a long time. Just as many Japanese gardens lead you from their entrance, through various meanderings, back to where you began, my encounters with Japan have led me back to a life that, like a garden itself, seems to hold within it an entire world.

I know why you have such a good time here," Eiko-san tells me when she invites me into her house for a farewell afternoon tea. "People like you here because when we usually meet Westerners from the United States, we think we have to change, be unlike ourselves, to be accepted by them. But with you, we just have to be ourselves."

I thank Eiko-san for her gift of an illustrated book of Bashō. Finally, I ask her something I have wanted to ask ever since moving in to my apartment: "Who are those two elderly Edo-period-looking women who sit on the shopping street all the time?"

Eiko-san laughs. "They do seem funny, don't they?"

I wonder if this is all Eiko-san will tell me. I sip my tea.

"They own the entire block," she continues. "They are the richest sisters in the area. When they go into the bank, they are greeted as if they are empresses."

"You're kidding. Their house looks like the worst in the neighborhood."

"Yes, this is true."

The day before departure, I revisit Sensō-ji. At Sensō-ji, the first fortune I received six months ago was No. 48 Small Fortune. Not knowing whether to keep it or tie it with the other fortunes in the trees, I kept it.

Now, I receive No. 28 Bad Fortune:

Although you are in a hurry, there will be no boat to cross the river. If you dare to sail, the boat will be swallowed by high waves.

You can't go ahead and should go back to your homeland. When you get home, you will not meet any crisis and your mind will be at peace.

*Your request will not be granted. *The patient is hard to get well, it will need a little time. *The lost article will not be found. *The person

you wait for will come but late. *Building a new house and removal are
both bad.

This time I decide to tie the white paper and leave it, with the countless
other fortunes, where it waits, for what I do not know, in a tree.

The morning of departure, I go to discontinue my cell phone service.
This has to be done in the store. Once I leave the store, I will no longer
be able to use my cell phone.

On the way, MM calls to say good-bye.

"You're the last one I'll talk to on this *keitai*," I tell him.

Leaving the store, I feel insecure without my working cell phone
accompanying me.

Walking down my neighborhood's shopping street, I see the two
elderly Edo-period-looking women. They are sitting, as usual, outside
their house. Before I get too close, I take out my camera and take a photo
of them. I'll send a copy of the photo to Eiko-san. "The richest sisters in
the area," I'll write on the back of the photo.

I practice saying good-bye to the man who sells roast chicken breasts
and potato croquettes on the corner. When I have readied what I want
to say, I go to the counter where he is sorting today's food display.

"*Kyo kaerimasu ni America*," I say. "*Domo arigato gozaimashita*." I
bow my head in thanks.

I walk the short distance from the shopping street to my apartment.
Eiko-san is outside. "The taxi will be here in a few minutes," she says.

I open the door to my apartment. On the step of the *genkan* is my
luggage, all ready to go.

At the taxi door, I thank Eiko-san and say good-bye. She takes a few
steps following the taxi.

The taxi takes me to Shinjuku, where I meet Mika before catching
the Narita Express for the airport. I tell her about the Bad Fortune I
received when I revisited Senso̅-ji yesterday.

Mika laughs.

"Why are you laughing?"

"Did you leave the fortune at the temple?"

"I sure did. But I wrote it down in my notebook."

Mika laughs again. "A bad fortune means that your luck can only get better."

"I'm going to miss you."

"I'll see you in February," she says, reminding me that I will see her when she comes to New York to sing the garden songs.

"I don't want to leave."

"It's okay. You have to leave so you can return."

II

Away

One

||||||||

Before

A friend who once lived in Japan tells me, "No matter how many Buddhas you've brought back with you, in the West you can't live the same life you lived in Japan."

Despite what my friend tells me, I still try.

After living in Tokyo, I don't want to live alone in Northampton, a small college town; I want to be near my close friends. I move to New York City. I see every possible Japanese film at the movies or on DVD and always check to see what's going on at the Japan Society. I find a place in midtown to eat *tonkatsu*, deep-fried pork cutlets, one of my favorite Japanese foods, and, even though it is winter, I keep Japanese iced barley tea in the refrigerator.

Ian and I get a subscription to BAM, so we know we'll see each other every month or so when he comes to New York. I go to DC to see him, and he shows me all the postcards and gifts I had sent him from Japan.

I continue to regale Ian with all things Japanese. Though Ian and I are back to talking every day on the phone, and neither of us has found someone to take each other's place in our lives, we now live in different cities. If we are to get back "together"—whatever that means—I know there are many obstacles, both logistical and emotional, with which we'd have to deal. Perhaps the relationship we're now having is the relationship we were meant to have all along?

When Brenda and I get together in a West Village café, she tells me that her Tokyo boyfriend, Taka, is waiting for a visa so he can be with her in the U.S. We talk for five hours—"Japan, Japan, Japan." When I introduce Ian to Brenda, he keeps asking her questions. He hopes she will explain to him the things I can't explain. When Brenda can't come up with satisfactory explanations, Ian sees that I'm not being difficult. There are so many things about Japan that can't be explained, especially from a Western point of view. "It just has to be experienced," Brenda tells him.

Although still wary of what he sees as my "romanticization" of Japan, Ian has an obvious affinity with what I share with him. When I introduce him to books I've read, he finds the same things I found in them. He is as excited as I am when I find him a book of the works of the Japanese art I admire, especially Kōrin's folding screens.

For his birthday, I give him a book of Kōetsu's calligraphy.

"When I first looked at the book, I thought it was something contemporary you were sending me," he says.

"The Japanese have been modern for ten centuries," I reply, quoting the French writer Henri Michaux. "It amazes me how the Japanese, like their culture, are somehow able to hold extremes in one frame. How else could a culture produce both kitsch and masterpiece?"

Ian comes to New York for Mika's concert. The moment Mika begins to sing, Ian grabs my arm, digging his nails into my skin. Despite the problems Mika has been having with her jaw, her voice is just as resonant as I heard it in Japan.

When the first song is over, I turn to Ian and whisper, "I told you."

At intermission, a middle-aged Japanese woman comes up to me. "I'm a friend of MM, his former student. I live in New Jersey, and MM asked me to come today to be here for him. I've heard so much about you, MM's writer friend, and am so glad to meet you."

At the reception after the concert, I meet in person for the first time Rahna Reiko Rizzuto, the writer I had contacted before I went to Hiroshima. A few days later, Reiko and I meet at the *tonkatsu* restaurant. And like I did with Brenda, we talk and talk and talk about Japan. In many ways, Reiko's life has changed even more dramatically than mine because of her time in Japan.

After returning from Japan, Reiko separated from her husband. They had been together since high school. Their separation was difficult due to their two sons, then four and six. But Reiko, like me, had discovered new parts of herself, new ways of being in the world during her time in Japan. She experienced this not in the neon-lit postmodern cultural hub of Tokyo but in the sleepier, provincial Hiroshima. This reassures me that my experience of Japan was not "romantic," as Ian claims.

At lunch, Reiko tells me of the many women she met in Hiroshima. It was difficult for these highly educated intelligent women to find their way in Japanese society, which does not make it easy for women to live independent, satisfying lives outside their roles of wife and mother.

"Kind of how I feel being back in the States. I don't know how to live a satisfying life in my own country," I say. "I never thought it would be easier to figure things out and manage for myself in Japan."

"My Japanese friends thought so differently than I was used to," Reiko says as we descend the subway stairs. "They got stumped when I asked them to compare things, to assimilate thoughts from various times or various fields. I was constantly asking why and they didn't understand my questions."

By the time we finish our conversation, many trains have come and gone. Finally, we part; I head uptown and Reiko heads to Brooklyn.

On my way home, I'm filled with an excitement similar to how I felt returning to my small Tokyo apartment. The more Reiko and I talked about Japan, the less alone in my experience I felt and the more I knew I had to find my way back to Japan.

I apply for a Fulbright to return to Japan. It will be many months until I hear if this will happen. I teach a disability studies course with a confidence I couldn't imagine a decade ago, a confidence reinforced by all the talks I gave on the subject in Japan. In the course, as I teach my students about how disability has been represented in Western culture, I know that although in Japan I found some of what I was looking for, I also know now I want to discover more of how disability appears in Japanese culture.

On my short New York City subway rides from my class to my apartment, I read my students' work. The train grinds to a halt. I look up and see we are stopped between stops, not at a station. The lights in the train blink off and on. In the Tokyo subway, I could not read any of the ads or understand much of anything I heard since I did not understand the language well enough. Back in a more familiar place, I'm not as interested in or aware of my surroundings.

Reaching my stop, I make sure I've taken everything with me. As I reach the turnstile, I reach into my front pocket for my wallet before realizing that in the New York City subway—the subway on which I have been riding since my childhood, the subway where I do not have to consult a map to reach my destination—that here, unlike in Japan, I do not need a ticket to exit the station.

I open the door to my apartment. Before leaving for Japan, I wondered how, without Ian, I would manage my loneliness in a place so different from what I was accustomed. I discovered this to be a misplaced fear. But now, I doubt myself in ways I thought I had put aside. How can I build a satisfying life by myself in the place I should feel is home? Why in New York City, where I'm busy all the time and among my closest friends, do I feel so alone?

In Japan I had put aside psychologizing. I refrained from figuring out people in the way we are accustomed to doing in the West. I befriended all kinds of people, let them be who they were without agonizing about why they acted, or didn't act, a certain way. It was enough just to pay attention. To observe. To be aware.

Up to now, during my time in New York, I have not been able to string together more than three dates with the same man. None develop into any kind of satisfying romantic relationship.

In Tokyo I didn't have what could be called a long-term relationship. Spending all those nights in GB, I likened myself to Christopher Isherwood during his time in Berlin. I saw and talked to friends or found just watching the transactions in the bar to be fascinating. Who might leave the bar with whom? Who will leave before the last train at midnight? Who will stay until the bar closes and perhaps spend the rest of the night in an Internet café waiting for the first morning train?

But now, in New York, I'm not interested in going to bars. The novelty of being single has worn off.

Late one night, closing the door on yet another man, old thoughts and feelings, until now dormant, surface. The clarity I felt about myself and my body has quickly been obfuscated in more familiar surroundings. Once again, I am psychologizing; I am Western, after all. It is as if I am once again in my early twenties, trying to figure out if, in fact, being disabled, I can attract men. Clearly, I am able to do so. But no sooner than I have attracted one, I need another, over and over, to prove, yet again, what I just thought I had proven to myself.

At least now this doesn't lead me into any harmful relationships, like it did when I was younger. I placate myself with this thought until another takes its place: I am becoming someone I do not want to be.

MM visits New York City. We have lunch with my parents, who come from upstate to see him. He tells my raised-in-Brooklyn Jewish mother she looks like Marilyn Monroe.

MM wants to see the exhibit on Jewish influence in entertainment at the Jewish Museum. His ebullient interest in a culture different from his own reminds me of what I miss about Japan.

Soon after his U.S. visit, I receive word from Japan that MM has had a stroke. He is in the hospital recovering; he still cannot speak. I want so much to write to him, but I am told he no longer uses e-mail. I contact the woman from MM's English-Speaking Union every few days to find out if there is any news about him. Finally, she tells me that MM is doing somewhat better. He is back at home but spends three days a week at a rehabilitation center. This makes things easier for his wife. He can understand what is said to him, in both Japanese and English, but he can barely speak a coherent word.

Being disabled my entire life, I have yet to experience the kind of loss that MM must feel. I can only imagine MM's frustration. His entire life has been built on communication.

One March day when I return home from teaching, I see a letter with the Fulbright insignia in the upper-left corner of the envelope. Standing in my apartment building lobby, I nervously open the envelope. I quickly read the letter: I have received a Fulbright.

Focus and purpose are restored. Now, I will have the opportunity to finish what I started in Japan. This time, will I see the big picture? Will I be able to see things as a seamless whole? This time in Japan, will I be of the "right mind" to see what I need to see? What might my next Sensō-ji fortune be?

My thoughts race ahead of me as I think of all I need to do before I return to Japan.

Two

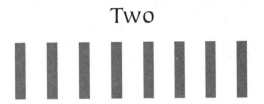

After

It starts with a dull pain in my upper-right side. When the pain stays for more than three days, I see Dr. Shay. Thinking this might be some sort of walking pneumonia, he prescribes antibiotics. The pain gets worse; I go back to the doctor. He changes course. A urine test shows some blood. Since I have a history of kidney stones, he calls to schedule a CT scan of my kidneys. But it is Friday, and no appointments are available until the middle of the next week.

Ian is scheduled to arrive in the morning. We have plans to drive upstate, spend Saturday night in Cooperstown, and visit the Baseball Hall of Fame before seeing Britten's *Death in Venice* Sunday afternoon. Dr. Shay says it's okay to go and prescribes Vicodin for the pain.

Ian picks me up, and I'm okay during the drive. We check into the motel, visit the Hall of Fame, and have barbecue for dinner. During dinner, the pain in my side increases.

"Are you okay?" Ian asks.

"It's a bit worse."

"You don't look good."

"I'll be okay." I think about my infected throat in Japan. I thought I'd be okay then, too. "You want to get some ice cream? There's a great place downtown."

We're walking down Cooperstown's Main Street eating our ice cream when the pain in my side gets sharper. Bending over, I drop the ice cream on the sidewalk. "Fuck."

"Are you okay?"

"I wanted that ice cream."

Ian laughs.

"Don't make me laugh," I say, holding my side.

Back in the motel, we watch an anime DVD. The pain isn't getting any better.

"I'm going to take a Vicodin." I reach for the pills I placed on the nightstand. "If I get loopy—" I take the pill instead of continuing. Ian will know what to do.

I fall asleep before the anime is over.

Did Boston or Cincinnati win?" I ask.

Nobody answers.

"Did Boston or Cincinnati win?" I ask again, a bit louder.

"What's going on?" Ian asks.

"I was watching the World Series and I don't remember who won."

"What?"

"The Red Sox or the Reds?"

"I don't know what you're talking about."

"Where am I?"

The next thing I know, there is light again. It takes me a few minutes to realize the sun is shining through the crack in the curtain. I see Ian, still sleeping on the other side of the bed. I remember that we're in a motel. In Cooperstown. I move a bit and my body feels flat, disconnected, as it does the morning after taking a sleeping pill, something I rarely do, only when it's impossible for me to sleep. I don't like being on drugs.

The pill bottle on the nightstand reminds me that I must have taken a Vicodin last night even though I have no memory of taking it.

"Are you okay?" Ian is awake.

"I don't know."

"You were very strange during the night."

"What did I do?"

"You thought you had been watching the 1975 World Series."

"The Red Sox versus the Reds?"

"Uh-huh."

"What happened?"

"The Reds won."

I begin to laugh, and the pain in my side returns.

I'm still woozy from the Vicodin. Tylenol gets me through a museum, lunch at a lakefront restaurant, and then *Death in Venice*.

When we return to the city in early evening, Ian drops me off at my apartment. "Call me and let me know how you're doing," he says before continuing on to Washington, DC; he has to go to work tomorrow.

Back in my apartment, I take my temperature. It's over 102°.

In the morning I call Dr. Shay to tell him about the fever. He says I should go to the emergency room. At least I could get the CT scan there and not wait until Wednesday. Remembering the over six-hour emergency room wait I had a year and a half ago when I had fever and was dehydrated, I wait in my apartment hoping the fever will lessen.

By late afternoon my fever reaches 104°. I call Dr. Shay to tell him I am going to the hospital. I take a taxi to the nearby emergency room.

Almost six hours later, I'm finally called from the waiting room, given IV fluid, and Torodol for the pain. I'm sent off for a CT scan.

Close to midnight I am told the CT scan showed nothing wrong with my kidneys. Because my fever remains very high, Dr. Shay wants me admitted to the hospital for observation.

Thankfully, Torodol relieves the pain. Another five hours later, I am wheeled up to what will be my hospital bed.

The hospital corridors are quiet and dimly lit by fluorescent lights. In my room I am helped into my bed. I try to be as quiet as possible. I do not want to wake the man who will be my hospital roommate, sound asleep on the other side of the curtain divider.

A woman appears. She drops a hospital gown on the bed and attempts to show me how to use the television remote.

I am not interested in the television. I am exhausted. Still feverish, I fall asleep without taking off my clothes.

In the morning, only a few hours since I arrived in my hospital bed, Dr. Shay makes his morning rounds. He has assembled a team of consultants: a urologist, an infectious disease expert, and a pulmonary specialist; he has scheduled various tests, including another CT scan, to get to the bottom of what is causing the pain in my side and the fever.

The lights are turned on and a young intern wakes me. A nurse follows him into the room.

"What's going on?" I ask.

"The CT scan you took earlier today showed some fluid in your lungs," the young doctor says.

"I thought that was a scan of my kidneys."

"Because of the fluid, we took another of your lungs, as well. You have two clots in your right lung."

"What?"

"We have to give you this injection—Heparin—to dissolve any other clots that might be on the way."

"But I don't have any trouble breathing." Then, I realize what the doctor has just told me. "What do you mean on the way?"

"Pulmonary emboli originate in the legs, usually the calves."

"I don't have calves," I tell this doctor, who has never seen my legs before. He has no idea what I'm trying to tell him.

The nurse is ready with the Heparin. She lifts up my T-shirt and injects the medication into my abdomen.

"That's not much fun," I say.

"Might as well get used to it," the nurse responds. "You'll probably have to inject yourself when you leave the hospital."

"Fat chance of that," I think but do not say out loud. My squeamishness about such things surely would make that a difficult proposition.

The clock tells me it is 2:00 a.m.

The lights in my room are turned on again. Once more my sleep is interrupted.

"Well," a blowsy blonde in a white doctor's smock is saying. This doctor looks like Kathleen Turner. A retinue of white-clad bright-eyed men and women surrounds her; my childhood experience in hospitals tells me they are medical students. "What you have killed sixty-thousand people in the United States alone last year."

"You've got to be kidding," I say. I'm not sure whether it's the statistic I'm reacting to or that this statistic is coming from a doctor who looks like a movie star. "But I don't have any trouble breathing." I repeat what I told the young intern in the middle of the night.

"Asymptomatic," she says as she checks my breathing with her stethoscope. "Unusual, but you also have some fluid in your lungs we'll have to drain."

"That doesn't sound pleasant."

"Just drill a small hole in your back, that's all." She has finished her examination and is about to leave. "You're a lucky guy."

The procession of medical students follows Kathleen Turner out of the room.

Dr. Shay arrives.

"I'm ordering some more blood tests, and an ultrasound to make sure there are no other clots developing."

"They develop in your calves. I don't have calves."

Dr. Shay laughs. He has a hearing impairment. He gets most of my disability references.

Before Dr. Shay departs, I want to learn all I can about pulmonary emboli from him.

More blood is taken, this time three vials, two of which have to be put on ice and sent to different labs across the country. "To check for rare clotting factors," Dr. Shay explains.

"I'm going to start a strong antibiotic in the IV. There's no agreement on whether you have incidental pulmonary infection, but it can't hurt. You're lucky they didn't cause any respiratory distress or loss of a limb. That is what often happens. Actually, I'm relieved."

"Relieved that I have blood clots in my lung?"

"Unexplained pain and fever had me thinking worse things."

"Worse things?"

"Cancer."

Late one afternoon, Reiko visits. She leaves her coat and backpack in the room; we walk the hospital hallway, first clockwise, then, for distraction's sake, counterclockwise. We're on our third perambulation around the hallway when, turning the corner to head back to my room, we see a red light blinking above my room.

My bed comes flying out of the room. The chair, with Reiko's coat and backpack, follow. Many nurses, doctors, and machines replace what used to be in my room.

"What's going on?" Reiko asks a passing nurse.

"Emergency," the nurse says before disappearing into the room.

The flashing red light flashes no longer. The doctors and nurses file out of the room. They huddle together, heads down.

A nurse I've gotten to know sees me and comes over. Her face looks stricken.

"Are you okay?" I ask.

"I was getting something for him, and when I came back he was dead."

"Dead?"

"Heart attack."

I hug the nurse.

I tell her that last night my roommate had been up most of the night. He was moaning and throwing up. When I asked him if he needed help, he told me no, he was okay. Should I have called the nurse anyway?

I notice a bed being removed from the room. My now-dead roommate is under the sheets that cover the bed.

A few minutes later, my bed and chair, as well as Reiko's coat and backpack, are taken back into the room.

"It's okay for you to go back in," the stricken nurse tells me. "If you want to change rooms, I'll see what I can do."

"That's okay." Though somewhat shocked—I've never before been in such close proximity to someone who has died—I'm more concerned for the nurse. "I should be fine."

"Are you sure?" Reiko asks when we return to my room.

"Yeah. I guess I'm sure."

In the room the dividing curtain remains drawn as if my roommate is still on the other side.

Later, in the evening, after I've eaten dinner and Reiko has left, I get out of bed. I go to the other side of the room. There is still no bed. Something shiny on the floor reflects the outside streetlight. I bend down and pick up a polished penny.

I think of how I usually leave a coin when I leave a room that has kept me safe during my travels. I think of how I doused the *jizu* statues

in the cemetery on Kōyasan before crossing the river to visit Kōbō
Daishi's grave. I realize that it must be Obon in Japan, where death is
treated as just another part of life.

What is causing my blood to clot? Will I be well enough to experience
Obon in Japan next August?

Closing my eyes, I imagine the soul of my dead roommate has returned to the place of his death in the guise of the penny.

After a week's stay in the hospital, my INR, the ever-changeable clot
rate, has reached the desired 2.0. I can go home.

Contrary to what that night nurse said, I will not have to self-
administer Heparin injections. I will take a daily dose of Coumadin.
Twice a week during the next few weeks, I will have to get my INR to
make sure I'm on the right dose. Since vitamin K counteracts Coumadin,
I will have to watch my intake of green leafy vegetables and other foods
with high vitamin K content. In a month, I will need a follow-up CT
scan to check on my lungs.

I am happy to be out of the hospital. But I am still more exhausted
than I've ever been. There's a lot I need to do if I am going to depart for
Japan on time. I need to find an English-speaking Tokyo doctor who
can continually monitor my INR.

A week later, the phone wakens me from an early evening nap. It's
Dr. Shay.

"You've tested positive for the anticardiolipin antibody," he tells
me.

"What?"

"One of the special tests we drew blood for when you were in the
hospital."

"What does it mean?"

"It means you'll have to be on blood thinners the rest of your life."

I am silent.

"You don't have lupus. The other tests came back negative."

In bed I stare at the ceiling. Until now, I thought my main medical concern throughout my life would be associated with my legs. Now, as I fall asleep, I imagine particles of my blood clotting and traveling throughout my body. Who knows when or where the next blood clot will appear?

My birthday is six days before I'm scheduled to leave for Japan. I spend the day with Reiko seeing an exhibit of Japanese photography. For lunch we eat *tonkatsu*.

I return to my apartment in the late afternoon. There's a message from Dr. Shay: the follow-up CT scan showed all was okay with the clots in my lungs. However, it also showed an enlarged spleen and numerous small lymph nodes in my lungs—two signs of HIV infection. He wants me to take an HIV test before I leave next week.

Quickly, I call Dr. Shay before he leaves the office.

"What does this mean?" I ask.

"It means you have an enlarged spleen and a bunch of small lymph nodes showing in your lungs. We need to check for the underlying cause."

"I can go get the HIV test in the morning. How long does it take for the results?"

"A day, if it's negative. The longer it takes, the more chance it's positive. They recheck a positive. We'll also do a T-cell count just in case we don't have the results back on Monday."

"I'm leaving on Wednesday."

"I know. I'll check for the results over the weekend. Come see me late Monday afternoon. Don't worry; you'll be fine."

I call Ian. I call Reiko. I call my parents.

The longer it takes, the more chance it's positive. It's not a good sign that I don't hear from Dr. Shay over the weekend. I don't sleep much and I take my antianxiety pills to slow down my quickly beating heart.

I'm on time for my Monday appointment with Dr. Shay. He calls me into his office.

"The results aren't back yet," he tells me as he sits behind his desk.

"That's not good news."

"And your T cells are 389. Not bad. But too low for the test to be negative."

As much as I had prepared myself for this moment, I now feel totally unprepared. A line has been drawn dividing my life into before what Dr. Shay just told me and after. I try to keep it together, but tears escape from my eyes.

How will I manage?

"How am I going to go to Japan?"

"On a plane."

"You mean I'm okay to go?"

"Your T cells are okay for now. There's nothing you can do here that you can't do in Japan. You'll have to test again in a month, and then T cells and a viral load every three months after that."

"I can do that." The tears have increased. "I'll be fine." I'm not sure if I'm trying to assure Dr. Shay or myself. "How did this happen?"

"There's no way of knowing how long you've been infected, but with your T-cell count, probably more than five years. It happens."

"I'm supposed to be happy right now. All I wanted was to go back to Japan."

"And you're going."

"What do I have to watch out for?"

"Besides checking your T cells and viral load, unexplained fever, swollen lymph nodes."

"What about those in my lungs?"

"We watch and wait and take another CT scan in a year."

"You're sure I can go to Japan?"

"Yes, I'm sure. As long as you get your blood work done. You know, right now you're more at risk from clotting than from HIV."

"Thanks."

Dr. Shay gets up from his desk. He has gone into his examination room and comes out with a syringe.

"What's that?"

"Pneumonia inoculation. Just to cover all the bases." He injects the syringe into my upper right arm. "Let me know how things are through e-mail."

He walks me out into the now-empty waiting room. The woman at the desk asks for the ten-dollar copayment.

"No copayment," Dr. Shay tells her. He hugs me and I leave the office.

Waiting for the elevator, I feel as if I have left a part of myself in Dr. Shay's office.

It seems like the minutes it takes the elevator to reach the lobby of the old medical building will never end.

The late afternoon sun glares. Instinctively, my right hand rises as if for protection. I see the Band-Aid Dr. Shay placed on my right arm to cover the site of the pneumonia inoculation. I don't feel safe. From what else do I need to be protected?

I am oddly disconnected from all the street activity that surrounds me. My life now feels sharply bifurcated into what was and what is. I don't want to think about what might be.

My cell phone rings. It's Ian.

"Not good news," I say before even saying hello.

"You're kidding."

"No. I wish I was."

"Oh, Kimba," he says, using his pet name for me.

"I need to take a taxi home. I'll call you later."

In the taxi I watch the rush hour streets crowded with people and cars. I watch but do not hear anything.

It is already dark when I return to my apartment. I still have to pack everything before leaving on Wednesday morning. I'm numb. But I know that underneath my emotional and physical exhaustion—only six weeks ago, I was in the hospital with two blood clots in my lung—I am more afraid than I've ever been.

I make a list of my close friends who I want to tell before I leave. I know this is a decision I will have to make time and again in the coming months: who to tell, when to tell, who not to tell.

I stare at the phone. I know that once I speak the words I know I will have to speak, I will have moved even farther away from what I used to think of as my life.

When I call my parents, my mother tells me she hadn't slept all weekend. I can tell my father is crying. I can only imagine what they will feel when their son, newly diagnosed, is halfway around the world.

A few hours later, I call them again to make sure my father is okay.

"Don't worry about me," he says. "Just do whatever you have to do and take care of yourself."

After talking with my father, I remember my last Sensō-ji fortune I received before leaving Japan: *Although you are in a hurry, there will be no boat to cross the river. If you dare to sail, the boat will be swallowed by high waves.*

Perhaps I shouldn't go.

But somehow, early Wednesday morning, I'm almost ready to leave.

Alone for the last time in the now-empty apartment, I go into the bedroom. I close my eyes. I take six deep breaths, in and out. I open my eyes. I take a penny from my pocket and place it underneath the radiator.

Another part of my life is done.

I close the front door and slip the keys under the door, just as I told my landlord I would do.

Downstairs, the car service to the airport has arrived. The driver puts my luggage in the trunk.

As we drive down the street, I lay my head back and close my eyes. I remember another part of the Sensō-ji fortune: *The patient is hard to get well, it will need a little time.*

For the first time since I first felt the pain in my side in August, some, just a bit, of the tension in my body is released.

Now, it's the end of September. I can't believe I'm finally on my way back to Japan.

III

World

"Promise me your love will never change," Sannojō said.
"It will never change."
"Promise never to forget me."
"I will never forget you."

Saikaku Iharu

One

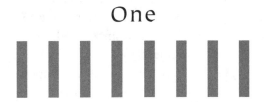

Survivals

Almost immediately after arriving in Tokyo, I flee the modern neon-lit city for Matsue, a small provincial city on the northwest corner of Honshu.

I have come to the place Lafcadio Hearn called the province of the gods: "The first of the noises of a Matsue day comes to the sleeper like a throbbing of a slow, enormous pulse exactly under his ear. It is a great soft, dull buffet of sound—like a heartbeat in its regularity, in its muffled depth, in the way it quakes up through one's pillow so as to be felt rather than heard."

Every morning since that day in Dr. Shay's office, what throbs and pulses, what quakes up through my pillow, is the knowledge of what is unseen yet detectable flowing in my blood. It waits to attack my body.

Hearn fled Tokyo. He came to Matsue, where "survivals" of an undisturbed old Japan were plenty, to find *kokoro*, the heart of old Japan. Matsue was the *before* Hearn wanted.

The foundations of my identity—being gay, being Jewish, being disabled—were set in motion at birth. Ever since finding out the test results in Dr. Shay's office, I have felt, for what seems like the first time, that my life has been split—now there is a *before* and an *after*.

Before taking another T-cell test, I have come to Matsue for a respite, in which I might begin to find my own *kokoro*, a new beginning to my new life.

When Hearn first arrived in Matsue, he lived in the small Tomitaya Inn, on the Ohashigawa. I cross the modern, no longer wooden, Matsue Ohashi Bridge. Now, where the inn once stood, there is only a small stone commemorative monument.

In November 1890 Hearn and his wife, Setsuo, moved to a traditional samurai house on a "very quiet street behind the mouldering castle." It was in front of this house that MM met Hearn's great-grandson. He told me this when he gave me a copy of *Kwaidan*. *It's a beautiful place with a small area still reminiscent of old Japan*, MM said.

Now preserved as Lafcadio Hearn's Old Residence, the front view of the house has not changed since Hearn immortalized it in "In a Japanese Garden." The day after I visit Izumo Taisha, I sit where Hearn once sat. In the tatami-matted reception room, I open the shoji on the south side of the room to take in the view of the garden: "Part of the O-Shiroyama, with the castle on its summit, half concealed by a park of pines, may be seen above the coping of the front wall, but only a part. . . . The shape of a very pretty garden, or rather a series of garden spaces, which surround the dwelling on three sides," compensates for what is blocked from view. Hearn assures that "from a certain veranda angle" a viewer "can enjoy the sight of two gardens at once."

Is there an angle from which to view my life as both before *and* after?

I get up and walk to the room that was used as both the dining room and Hearn's bedroom. In his study, simply furnished with a writing desk and a chair near the veranda, there is no decoration. In these rooms, Hearn began work on two of his most famous books, *Glimpses of Unfamiliar Japan* and *Kwaidan*.

What is the book I most need to write?

The book about disability in Japan is the book I came to write.

Now, with all that has changed, it seems there is another, more urgent book to write, a book where I am more subject than researcher. Is there a connection between the two?

Opening another shoji, I see the second garden with its lotus pond. Hearn delighted in watching every phase of the "marvelous growth" of the lotus plants, "from the first unrolling of the leaf to the fall of the last flower." The Japanese garden, like Japan itself, is more a process than a result. And this process, despite its seemingly unceasing progress from a wooden bridge to a metal bridge, leaves a remnant, a memory, in its wake.

I go next door to the Memorial Museum. In the museum is Hearn's favorite writing desk, taller than usual, specially designed so he could better use his one good eye. In a vitrine nearby, I find the telescope Hearn always kept at his desk to help him see, as well as the magnifying glass he used when walking outside.

Would this idyllic quarter still remain if Hearn hadn't lived here?

In the small, well-preserved samurai district surrounding the Hearn residence, I eat *warigo soba*, the local noodle specialty. I once again think of MM—how we enjoyed eating noodles together, how when he first told me about Matsue, he said, *Maybe I will go with you. I would like to return to Matsue.* Though I know I will see MM in Tokyo, I mourn the occasion that never came to be.

That night at the *ryokan*, I hear the sound of drums outside. I look out the window across the train tracks. I see the canal but can't see from where the sound comes.

Then, I remember the *ryokan* keeper told me local teenagers were practicing for the upcoming festival.

Before going to sleep, in my journal I write: "The sound of the festival drums reminds me that I need to find what pulses underneath the life I have returned to live in Japan. Remember these days when my health was fine and I visited the Lafcadio Hearn sites in Matsue and Izumo Taisha."

On the way back to Tokyo, I stop overnight in Kyoto. I visited the temple at Kiyomizu-dera on my first trip to Kyoto; this time my priority is different.

The next morning I'm up at 7:00 a.m. I eat a quick breakfast and take a taxi to Kiyomizu-dera's temple grounds. I've never been here so early, before the tourists overwhelm the temple.

This time I'm not here to see the temple. Nor am I here to walk between the two rocks at the lovers' shrine. I don't even enter the temple. I walk on the side of the hill until I reach Otawa-no-taki, the waterfall.

According to legend, Enchin, a Nara priest, had a vision in which he was told to look for the clear water origin of the Yodo River. Instead, he found Gyoei, an old hermit, sitting on a log. Gyoei told Enchin he had been sitting for two hundred years reciting invocations to the merciful Kannon. He wanted Enchin to take his place while he made a pilgrimage to the mountaintop. He suggested that the log on which he had sat would make good material for building an image of Kannon.

Gyoei never returned.

Enchin searched for him. When he found only a pair of shoes lying on the summit of the nearby mountain, he realized the old hermit had been, like in the denouement of many of the stories told in Noh, none other than Kannon himself. Gyoei had returned to heaven.

Enchin returned to sit on the log. As he had been told, he tried to fashion an image of Kannon from the log. For twenty years Enchin could not figure out how to shape the log into the image of Kannon.

One day the warrior Tamuramaro was hunting for a stag. Tamuramaro found Enchin in the woods. With Tamuramaro's help, Enchin finally transformed the log into the image of Kannon. Impressed with Enchin's devotion, the warrior dismantled his own house, reassembling it as a temple beside the nearby waterfall.

This early in the morning, there is no line of tourists waiting to drink the healing spring water.

I bring the long, metal pole closer to my mouth. I take a deep breath before I drink the cold, clear water from the pole's metal cup. I swallow the water and imagine I feel it cleansing my body of what needs to be cleansed.

Back in Tokyo, I go to draw blood for the T-cell test.

After leaving the clinic, I roam through Kappabashi, kitchen town, where restaurants find most of their wares. Walking down the main avenue about a half block away, I see what seems to be a jeweler or gem store. I wonder what a jewelry store is doing in Kappabashi.

Getting closer to the store, I see the windows are filled with what now seem to be brightly colored cakes.

When I reach the store, I burst out laughing. I've been seeing, first from afar and now up close, a store filled with the brightly colored plastic food usually displayed outside restaurants, showing what is served inside. Originally made from wax in the nineteenth century, these plastic replicas were increasingly used in the decades following the U.S. occupation when foreign foods were introduced to the puzzled Japanese. These uncannily realistic mock-ups are godsends for those *gaijin* who, like me, can't read a Japanese menu.

Looking at the store filled with fake food makes me hungry. It is time to meet Mika for lunch.

It is so good to see Mika again. She tells me she will perform my garden songs in a concert in Yokohama.

"How is your jaw?" I ask.

"I've been working with a healer, so it seems stronger."

Mika has never mentioned a healer before. And if she had mentioned a healer before, I doubt it would have intrigued me as much as it does now.

After lunch, Mika and I go to Sensō-ji. A visit to Sensō-ji is something I've both feared and anticipated since I knew I would return to Japan. I hear the rattling of the wooden fortune sticks in their metal boxes. As we approach the temple, the rattling gets louder and louder.

I stand in front of the wooden drawers, each marked with the characters that correspond to the fortunes. I shake the metal box. "I'm nervous," I admit to Mika.

"You've become very superstitious," she says.

Mika has no idea what makes me so nervous. I wonder if she notices how much I'm sweating. With most people not yet knowing what's going on inside my body, I've become more like the Japanese. I now have both a public life and a private life. It is becoming apparent that I will soon need to reconcile these two lives.

A wooden stick escapes from the metal box's narrow hole. I match the kanji on the stick with the characters on the drawer. I open the drawer and remove the paper fortune:

Relying on a person in a higher rank for help to succeed in one's life is just like a cock tries to fly following a phoenix and perches on a higher twig.

Polling a boat across the stream is a simile of your getting along well with others in this world.

You will rise in the world and be wealthy.

*Your wish will come true, so you should be modest for everything. *The sick person will get well. *The lost article will be found. *The person you are waiting for will come. *Building a new house and removal are both good. *It is good to make a travel. *Both marriage and employment are good.

I am more than relieved. Somehow, I have chosen—or have I been given?—No. 96 The Best Fortune.

I want to show you a little something," Mika says after we leave Sensō-ji.

Where is she taking me? From my time spent with Mika, I've learned these "little somethings" are usually the highlights of my time with her.

"Here we are," she tells me in front of a café. Inside the café she introduces me to Izumi. "She runs the gallery, Gallery-ef."

Gallery? What gallery? I don't see a gallery.

The twenty- or thirtysomething Izumi—it is still difficult for me to tell how old a Japanese person might be—leads us to the back of the small café. We are in a narrow passage, and the floor is now gravel.

We pass through a small, open doorway and stand in a small *genkan*. Above us is a narrow, two-storied room. The floors are lacquer.

"It was an Edo-period *kura*, a storehouse," Izumi explains. "When my grandfather died, my family was supposed to sell it for the funeral money. But we got together and, because the building survived both the 1923 earthquake and the war bombings, we decided we should keep it. A friend constructed the lacquer floors, and we converted the warehouse into a gallery." She points to a black-and-white photo on the *genkan* wall. The photo shows the *kura*, the only building still standing among the postwar ruins.

I think of the young MM. He lived in this part of town during the war. Somehow, he also survived.

This old *kura*, transformed by a lacquered contemporary loftlike façade that also preserves what was, also makes me think of Ian. He must see this place when he comes to visit in February. His large pencil drawings would be perfectly shown in this place that somehow survived both natural and manmade disasters.

On the way to the subway, on a street twice destroyed, I think about the T-cell results for which I am waiting. I am filled with questions: What survives? Who survives? How long will I survive?

That night, I am back in my tiny room. I chose to live in a "managed apartment" because it is only a short taxi ride to my English-speaking doctor.

Lying on my narrow single bed, I think about Gallery-ef. Because of

Izumi and her family, the old building has a new life. Still thinking about survival, I remember three stories I heard shortly after 9/11.

A blind man interviewed on television tells the first story. He sits with his guide dog at a small round table across from the interviewer. The man, probably a bit older than fifty, tells the interviewer how his dog led him down the stairs after the first plane hit. Despite the chaos, the dog did his job, leading his master out of the burning and collapsing World Trade Center building.

"The dog must have been frightened," the interviewer asserts. "Or agitated."

"I don't know what the dog felt, *if* the dog felt. My dog is trained to do his job, and that's what he did."

I know I read the second story but I can't remember where I read it. A woman in one of the towers was injured. Someone—a fireman? a co-worker? I don't remember—found her and began to lead her down the stairs. Even though she knew time was running out, even though her would-be rescuer kept telling her there was no time to stop, the pain in the woman's leg forced her to stop. She could not go on without resting; she stopped with the rescuer on a stairway landing near a doorway.

While they waited on the landing, the stairway beneath them burst into flames and began to collapse. The rescuer grabbed her and pushed her through the doorway. They found another intact stairway, which led them to safety.

"If she hadn't stopped to catch her breath, if she hadn't been injured and her leg didn't hurt as much as it did, we would have both been on that burning stairway. We would have died for sure when it collapsed," the rescuer said.

The third story is one I heard when I called a friend in New York to find out how he was doing.

"As soon as the first plane hit, a guy who worked in the tower got out. He called his boyfriend, who worked a few blocks away, and told him to meet on a nearby corner. The reunited lovers embraced on the corner and started to walk away from what was quickly turning into smoldering rubble. A moment later, the guy who worked in the tower realized his lover was no longer walking at his side. He turned around. Some debris had fallen from a building, hit his lover's head, and killed him."

Over the years, I've learned that my disability experience forces to the surface what everyone—disabled and nondisabled alike—prefers to keep tightly wrapped inside.

Now, this situation has expanded. I don't yet know how to keep things in balance: none of us know when or how we will die. As we live our lives, most of us do not think about this very much. Now, I think about it all the time.

Finally, the results are in: 361. Almost the same as what they were a month ago, before I returned to Japan. I e-mail Dr. Shay. He tells me now we can wait three months, until after the new year, for both a new T-cell test and a test for the viral load. In the meantime, for additional protection, he suggests I get a hepatitis A and B vaccine, as well as a flu shot.

Walking in my new neighborhood, I think about how I've begun to measure my life from test to test, in month-to-month increments. Though waiting for the test results is nerve-wracking, receiving the results, at least this time, seems anticlimactic.

Already, Japan has once again taken me both outside of myself and deeper into myself—how this happens simultaneously, I do not know. I only experience this here. Perhaps what is ahead won't be as difficult as I think it will be?

But now I know another test begins. As I walk up the hill to my room, I know I will eventually have to tell my Japanese friends what is going on.

I stop at the small local shrine and make an offering. I ring the shrine bell, bow, and clap, sending my prayers wherever they are welcomed.

It is the end of October. The gods are still at Izumo Taisha. Closing the metal door to my room, I feel decidedly, yet thankfully, alone.

Two

A Pair of One-Winged Birds

How Matsui Ryosuke became my Fulbright advisor is a typical Japanese story. Nagase wrote the invitation letter necessary to receive a Fulbright. He was supposed to serve as my advisor. But my grant was to be until the end of June, and Nagase's contract with his university went only until the end of March, which meant the university would not let him serve as my advisor. So, Nagase suggested Matsui-sensei to the Fulbright office. Matsui-sensei, on Nagase's recommendation, agreed.

When I meet Matsui-sensei, I initially think of it as a formality. Since I began the research during my previous stay in Japan, I don't think I'll need much guidance. The gentle, sixty-five-year-old social welfare professor surprises me at our first meeting in his university office by asking, "What is your research and writing schedule?"

"What?" is the only reply I can muster. I've never kept to a research or writing schedule. Realizing Matsui-sensei doesn't know me or the work I've done, and that it's best I prove to him I'm serious about my work, I show him an article I've written.

This, and our ensuing conversation about my previous research in Japan, does the trick. Soon, Matsui-sensei, a former government bureaucrat who is also president of the Japan Society for the Rehabilitation of

Persons with Disabilities (JSRPD), is providing valuable contacts and inviting me to seminars on topics, such as international development and disability, I know little about. Eventually, he asks me to speak not only to his classes but also at conferences. Matsui-sensei helps me hire one of his graduate students to do some research for which it is necessary to read Japanese. He also invites me to his home and introduces me to his family.

Most importantly, Matsui-sensei asks the JSRPD staff to arrange a meeting with Hanada Shuncho, the person who finally might inform me of Ebisu's disability and religious pedigree.

I also want to further the song-cycle project with Mika. Two more songs have been written. Mika will premiere them as part of a concert in Tokyo in December. Knowing I also want to find a way to have the poems printed, Mika introduces me to a young calligrapher who decides to design a Japanese *tenugui*, a traditional cloth towel, using the poems. Mika also arranges for me to sit in on rehearsals for Mikami Kayo's upcoming butoh performance.

Professionally, everything seems set to move forward. But internally, beneath the surface, I know my body is engaged in battle. As Dr. Shay told me in his office just a short time ago, there's no way of knowing when the virus entered my body. All I know is that in 1988, when Alex tested positive, I tested negative. Since then, safer sex has been my norm. In my head, I play over and over again all the sex I can remember—was it *then*? Was it *him*? I scour my memory for the times I had an unexplained fever, felt fluish, or had any clue to my body's reaction to the virus's initial invasion.

But these questions, like when I was younger and asked myself countless times why I was born with the body I was born with, are a waste of time. And time—not knowing how long I might remain healthy—is something of which I am now all too aware. I know my second stay in Japan cannot be the same as my first. Being disabled since birth, I'm used to being different. But this time the difference cannot be seen.

I think about Rafael, now back in Venezuela, telling me he wanted to leave Japan, to return home, where he could feel as if he, once again, belonged, a feeling I had never felt at home or abroad.

But during my first stay in Japan, I felt attractive in a way I had rarely felt before. Now, even though on the outside nothing has changed, I feel like damaged goods. A hidden difference now resides, invisible, within me. Not a flattering, comfortable, or comforting way to feel.

A relationship seems farther away than at any other time during my life. Since returning to Japan, I've yet to go to the bars in Nichōme. The bars are not easy to get to from where I'm now living. But I know that's not the reason I've yet to go. I'm not ready to tell men I've just met what I would need to tell them. But at night, when I'm in my room, I do go online.

One night in early November, I see the profile for a thirty-one-year-old guy in Sapporo, a city I've been fascinated by ever since watching the 1972 Winter Olympics on TV. Sapporo holds the famous Yuki Matsuri, the snow festival, every February.

"I've always wanted to go to Yuki Matsuri," I write in a message I send to the guy in Sapporo.

Quickly, he responds, "If you get up to Sapporo, I'd love to show you around."

These are the first words Mike and I exchange.

Two weeks later, after speaking on the phone every night since we exchanged those messages, he is on a plane to Haneda Airport. Mike, a Canadian who has been teaching English in Sapporo for the past fifteen months, has never been to Tokyo before.

I meet Mike at the airport early on a Sunday morning. He is dressed in a greenish-gray business suit. "Better chance of an upgrade," he tells me.

Mike is six feet tall, wide shouldered, and muscular from his kendo. It was kendo, and the experience of his ex who taught English in Japan, that spiked Mike's interest in Japan. After his ex unexpectedly ended their nine-year relationship, only three months after they bought an apartment together, Mike figured it was time to go to Japan. He applied for two teaching jobs, got one, and extended his contract another year in August.

I have told Mike about my disability, but that doesn't lessen my anxiety of meeting him in person for the first time. Three dimensions are much different than photos and talking on the phone. We have talked about the risk of our plan to spend the next three days together, spending the night in my tiny room and even tinier single bed.

What we have not yet talked about is the virus. Everything I've read recommends not telling anyone you do not know well over the phone. Still, I feel a bit guilty for not telling him. What if he has come all this way and has no interest in someone living with HIV?

As I escort Mike back to my room via three trains, I try to match his by-now-familiar phone voice with his dark-brown eyes, hidden by narrow, rectangular glasses. His head is square, his nose is flat, his cheeks are high. "Somewhere I have Cherokee in my family," he says, smiling his slightly goofy smile, brightening his difficult-to-read, serious demeanor.

Emerging from the train station near my place, Mike stops on the corner.

"What's wrong?" I ask.

"I think I've seen more *gaijin* since we got off the train than I've seen my entire time in Sapporo," he says.

When we arrive in my room, we sit together on my bed. He kisses me.

"This is going to be a fun few days," he says before kissing me again.

We spend the afternoon visiting Meiji Jingu and shopping in Harajuku. Not only does Mike want to spend as much time as I do in Kiddieland but he also knows all the anime characters in the store. He finds small, pale-colored bears on whose paw feet different birthday months are printed; he buys one pale-blue May for himself and one pale orange for my September. Walking out of the store, he shows me how each bear has magnetic paw hands, so the bears can, in their way, hold hands.

Throughout the day, Mike is very silent, so it's difficult to know what he's thinking. This makes me nervous; every so often, I check in with him to make sure he's okay. "Oh, yes," he assures me. "I'm just taking it all in." I remember that Mike has never been off the northern island of Hokkaido during his time in Japan. I tell myself to stay in the moment and not to worry about how it's going or about what I still need to tell Mike before we sleep together tonight.

For dinner, I take Mike to my favorite tempura restaurant in Shinjuku. After our dinner, Mike pays at the cashier. "I've got this," he tells me.

I walk with Mike through Nichōme and take him to GB, the first time I have been since returning to Japan.

"Ginger ale," the bartender says, remembering my drink.

"I'm noticeable," I say to Mike. I'm both somewhat proud and somewhat embarrassed that I've been remembered. "I used to spend a lot of time here when I was in Japan the first time."

Back in my room, we undress. We are naked in my single bed. Mike starts to kiss me.

"Wait," I say. "There's something I have to tell you."

Mike lifts himself off me. He looks at me, waiting to find out the reason for this interruption.

I take a deep breath before I say, "I'm HIV positive." I turn away.

"That's okay," I hear Mike say. "I know how to have safe sex."

He starts kissing me again.

I put my palms on his chest, gently pushing him away so I can see his face. "Are you sure?"

Mike starts kissing me again.

The next night we ascend the tower at Roppongi Hills to Tokyo City View. Mike snaps photos of the nighttime panorama from the fifty-second floor of the building. On the clear window, I trace the twilit city's major thoroughfares and see some of my favorite sites from this unfamiliar perspective. The rambunctious, always-in-motion city moves more slowly from up here. The lights flicker like fireflies. I visualize each as the virus that replicates, wreaking its havoc as it courses through my defenseless body.

Looking at the flickering lights, I imagine the countless random encounters happening below and think of the randomness of meeting Mike—all that had to happen, and not happen, to lead us at the same time on the same night to be at our separate computers in separate cities on our separate islands in different parts of a country neither of us call home.

Soon, the sky darkens. All the lights—from the buildings, neon signs, and cars—mark effortless pathways through what I know to be a city daunting to navigate. From this height above the city, what awaits around the corner, at the next subway stop, in neighborhoods far beyond, is visible, discernible by following the lights with your eyes.

If only I could know what awaits me, what awaits my body, what awaits Mike and me.

When we've finished our 360-degree tour of nighttime Tokyo, Mike shows me the photos he's taken from City View. He also shows me photos he has surreptitiously taken of me tonight and throughout our first days together.

Mike has to leave this afternoon to catch his plane back to Sapporo. "Do you know about the love plan?" he asks.

"The love plan?"

"We're both on Vodafone," he says, referring to our Japanese cell phone provider. "You choose one number and pay only 300 yen each month for unlimited calls to that number. We should do it. This way we can talk as often and for as long as we want for only 300 yen each month."

Mike lingers with me in bed for as long as he can before he has to leave for the airport.

No sooner have we said good-bye and he is on his way than my cell phone signals that I have a new text message: "I had such a fun time. I can't wait till I see you again."

During the next few weeks, Mike and I develop a routine, something easier to do with him than it was with the more mercurial Ian.

Every night when Mike calls, it is also time for me to take the blood thinner I'll have to take for the rest of my life. Since I've been in Japan, my clot rate has been too low, probably because green tea counteracts the blood thinner. My current dosage has risen from five to eight milligrams: one five-milligram pill and three one-milligram pills.

As I talk to Mike, I take out the pills. I am about to put them in my mouth when Mike asks, "What's wrong?"

"I accidentally took out three five-milligrams and one one-milligram instead of the other way around. I was about to take sixteen instead of eight milligrams of the blood thinner."

"You have to be careful."

"I know. I could have bled to death."

"Please don't do that."

"I'll do my best."

During these nightly calls, we plan for him to return to Tokyo for Christmas and stay through New Year's. In Japan everything closes between December 29 and January 3, so Mike is off from work for an extended time.

There's nothing quite like a Tokyo Christmas. Right after Halloween, all kinds of lights, and I mean all kinds, are brought out. Department stores, public plazas, and shop windows are decked out for a holiday that, to the Japanese, means *kaimono matsuri*, a shopping festival. Christmas Eve is a romantic holiday in Japan. Even those who are single leave work early that night so their colleagues won't know they will spend the night alone. The lines at the subway ticket machines on Christmas Eve are the longest of the year. This year it is doubly so since Christmas Eve falls on a Saturday night. But if Christmas Day wasn't on Sunday, as it is this year, it would be a normal workday in Japan.

As soon as Christmas is over, all the Christmas-related displays are immediately whisked away, replaced by the traditional Japanese New Year's decoration of pine and bamboo. It is as if Christmas never happened. Now, it is time for the more reflective, if still festive, Japanese tradition to take center stage.

This year's calendar also has Hanukkah, the Jewish holiday, coinciding with Christmas. I like to celebrate by lighting the candles and exchanging a gift on each of the holiday's eight nights. I'm excited that this year I will get to spend these days with Mike in Tokyo.

When Mike arrives we easily settle in my small Tokyo room. Never has a space in Tokyo seemed so intimate.

I introduce Mike to the blessings over the Hanukkah candles. I tell him I used to call my aging paternal grandmother to sing the blessings for her over the telephone on the first night of Hanukkah. "I will live another year to hear you sing the *baruchas*," she told me.

I introduce Mike to my friends, including Mika. Everyone likes easygoing Mike. They also see how happy I am being with him.

We spend New Year's Eve at a party hosted by Mika. The party includes an eclectic mix of Japanese and *gaijin*, including Donald Richie, whose writings guided me during my first stay in Japan. I'm relieved to know that I don't have to worry about Mike, who is garrulous enough to fend for himself at such a gathering.

Just after midnight, Mika serves soba, a Japanese New Year's tradition symbolizing a long life. Only Mike knows how much this ritual means to me.

Then, all of us make our way to the local shrine. We line up to receive the traditional cup of saké, which has been blessed by the shrine's high priest. We notice that dogs accompany many of those who wait with us in line. "It's the Year of the Dog," Mika informs us.

"Does that mean for next year's Year of the Pig, people will bring pigs to the shrine?" I ask Mike.

"And what happens during the Year of the Tiger?"

Standing in the saké line, I realize that Mike has learned what I learned during my first stay in Japan: he accepts when Japanese do things that don't quite make sense to Westerners.

On New Year's Day, we walk around Daikanyama and are surprised to find most of the stores and cafés open. We take a break at a café. After we've ordered and been served, I look across the table at Mike.

Unlike other times when I've met a special man, this time I have not let go of the life I was living at the time I met him. Even though Mike and I talk every night on the phone, even though I excitedly anticipate the next time I will see him, I have kept up with my research, participated in the two concerts Mika has given of the new songs, kept going out to spend time with my Tokyo friends. I've tried, and been mostly successful at, not predicting what the future may or may not be.

"What are we?" I ask Mike.

"We're boyfriends," he says.

"Boyfriends," I say, part statement, part question. "What does that mean to you?"

"It means we have a commitment to each other."

"Commitment? What does that mean?"

"It means that when I say I'm going to call you, I will call you, unless something comes up, and then I'll call you to tell you I'm not going to be able to call you."

I smile at his simple, direct answer.

The next day Mike will leave in the afternoon. He knows we will see each other in five weeks, when I've planned to come up to Sapporo for Yuki Matsuri. But he seems sad. As the time nears for him to leave for the airport, he begins to cry. Wordlessly, I wipe his tears from his face.

Just like the last time he left, no sooner is he out the door than I receive a text message from him: "The past ten days were the happiest days of my life. I'll call you when I get home tonight."

My return message tells him I feel the same: "I can't wait to see you again."

The person you are waiting for will come. Since finding out I was HIV positive, I didn't think a relationship could be possible. Among the numerous surprises Japan has given to me, Mike is perhaps the biggest surprise of all.

It couldn't be as easy as this, could it?

The day after Mike's departure, it is time for me to go to the medical clinic to draw blood for my next T-cell count.

Three

History Being Created, or
What the Leech Child Says

Finally, Ebisu.

Ebisu is an area of Tokyo I never encountered during my first stay in Japan. Going to and from my new apartment, I often have to change train lines at a station named Ebisu. When the train doors open and close, the merry Ebisu beer jingle plays on the station platform. Outside the station, I see my first three-dimensional representation of Ebisu, the jolliest of the *shichifukujin*, the Seven Lucky Gods of Japan.

Thanks to Matsui-sensei, I will finally meet Hanada Shuncho, the disability studies scholar who says Ebisu is disabled. In preparation, I ask my research assistant to translate "History Is Being Created," Hanada-sensei's article Matsui-sensei has given to me. In the chapter, Hanada-sensei relates a Japanese creation myth.

After giving birth to the sun and the moon, Izanagino-ko and Izanamino-mikoto, the Japanese version of Adam of Eve, bore a baby whose lower body was paralyzed. He could not speak a word. This child was called Hiru-ko, alluding to Hiru, a leech that roamed the rice paddies and sucked the blood of humans and animals. After Hiru-ko was three years old, still unable to stand upright, he was set to sea on a small boat. His parents abandoned their child; they devoted their life to nation building. The child was never given the name of Mikoto as proof of his divinity. At the places where this boat is said to have arrived to shore are shrines that use the kanji for Hiru and Ko. These kanji are now read as Ebisu. By the middle of the Edo period, Ebisu became the most popular of the *shichifukujin*.

The *shichifukujin* appear in early collections of senryu, short poems consisting of seventeen syllables. In one senryu, it is written that six of the *shichifukujin* are all *katawa*, which means incomplete but can also mean distorted or disabled. In this senryu, only Benten, the one female deity, is nondisabled. However, Hanada-sensei says later myths describe her as having a sexual abnormality that the Japanese are too embarrassed to mention in detail.

Thus, the gods who are supposed to bring about *fuku*, fortunes, are the gods with *fugu*, distortion and disability. Fortunate distortion. A good description of my experience of Japan.

I meet with Hanada-sensei at the offices of JSRPD. He is accompanied by Aeio-san, a graduate student who is familiar with his teacher's unique speech. During our meeting, Aeio-san serves as Hanada-sensei's interpreter. There is also an interpreter to translate into English from Japanese.

Hanada-sensei was born in 1945 with cerebral palsy. Sitting across from me in his wheelchair, he seems frail. His large-framed glasses accentuate his thin face. His arms are akimbo, each loosely bent over each arm of his wheelchair. Hanada-sensei's languid speech initially sounds as if it is a recording playing in slow motion. But after a short while, I easily recognize its musical rhythm, which is often interrupted by bursts of laughter.

I ask Hanada-sensei, "Do people realize that when they pray to Ebisu, they are praying to a disabled god?"

"Most of the statues of Ebisu show him holding a fishing rod and usually show him sitting not quite right, neither standing nor walking. The lesson I learned from Ebisu, from Ebisu fishing without moving, is that it's better not to move."

"Do you think everybody gets that lesson from Ebisu or just you?"

"Ebisu is holding the fish. But he has a disability in his legs. Maybe he is paralyzed, so in order to fish he should stay in one place."

By now, I've become accustomed to these kinds of indirect answers.

"In the Edo era, the thirteenth shogun, Iesada, had CP. Also, the Maeda family, the strong power, had a disabled son. The Date family warrior, Date Masamoe, was called Dokuganju, the one-eyed dragon. And the Toyotomi clan has Yoshitsugu Ōtani with leprosy. Historically, Japan has been an agricultural society. The basic lifestyle is living in the community. People who are rare—different—are accepted.

"This is also the case with *bakemono*. In Japan the border between the present world and the *bakemono* world is not so big. There is much interaction between the present world and the *bakemono* world. Tree is tree, but in this tree, the *bakemono* is living, the place where gods and the souls live. Everyday goods are also where the gods, the souls, are living. *Shamoji*, the rice scoop when you eat rice—in that kitchen tool there is also living the soul."

"Why are most of the *biwa hōshi* blind?"

"This goes back to Semimaru, one of the great one hundred poets. In Japan there has been a structure where people do the same thing for their entire life. One of the jobs for disabled people has been artistic, like playing a musical instrument. As in the *Heike monogatari*, the disabled have created the Japanese language."

"How did you come to learn all this?"

"I was thinking what people with disabilities don't do. I was thinking there are very few people who are studying disability. I was thinking to become an expert in some area. I was born disabled. I don't know any other life. What I can do is limited, but I can concentrate on what I do.

Speech. Communication is difficult. I have a speech difficulty. It is difficult to communicate. That might be the big issue."

I wait until I am sure Hanada-sensei has finished and all his words have been translated before I tell him, "I often ask myself why someone who is not disabled should care about any of this. Your work shows that disability, even when unseen or unacknowledged, is a part of life, part of everything. You tie disability to so many aspects of life, it's so much more than disability. And to find that here in Japan is very special to me."

Leaving my meeting with Hanada-sensei, I have more of an idea of the multiple dimensions of disability in Japanese culture. But I remain perplexed.

I was born disabled. I don't know another life. Until a few months ago, Hanada-sensei's words would have also been true of my life.

What both Hanada-sensei and I share is a kind of difference that, despite all the barriers thrown in our way, hasn't precluded our participation in the society at large. But what about those without the tools with which we've been privileged, most notably education? And even with education, most would remain unexposed to true images of themselves in their own culture.

I think about how in most cultures, because of the lack of teachers who are disabled, there is no tradition of handing down disability history from one generation to the next.

My thoughts turn to Fukushima-sensei, the deafblind professor whom I met at the University of Tokyo's Barrier-Free Project during my first stay in Japan. For Fukushima-sensei, it was learning touch-Braille, a means of communication, that opened the world to him and opened him to the world.

What is it like to be disabled in Japan? That koan-question, which has followed me throughout my days in Japan, is raised once again. It is a complex question, one of experience, not of resolution.

The Ebisu beer jingle reminds me it is time to change trains. As I pass the Ebisu statue, I now see Ebisu as a disabled god. Hanada-sensei is right—Ebisu does not sit quite right. This reminds me that the stories we choose to tell, and pay attention to, are central to how we think of ourselves and our place in the world.

Soon, I will have to figure out a way to communicate to the world about the new difference that has entered my life.

I visit MM at the Yokohama daycare center where he spends three days a week. MM is waiting just beyond the door for my prearranged arrival. I miss my outings with MM very much—noodles, as well as Japan itself, are not the same without him. When I first enter the daycare center, I see his beaming smile. His body almost jumps out of his wheelchair. He is very happy to see me.

When he speaks, he struggles after more than a few words; his frustration is palpable.

But he still understands both Japanese and English. I tell him about my research. I have begun to find more representations of disability in Japanese culture, a process that began with MM mentioning Hōïchi and giving me a copy of Hearn's *Kwaidan*. I tell him what I saw on my trip to Matsue and how much I would have enjoyed eating *warigo soba* with him.

When, after his few words, speech does not arrive, he actively nods his head to show his agreement. He holds my hand.

Before leaving, he gives me a booklet. It is the compilation that his friends put together in honor of his seventy-fifth birthday, for which I contributed my story of first meeting MM at the I-House.

On the train, I read what another friend of MM has written about MM's interest in cross-cultural humor: MM's friend accompanied him to a "Doing Business in Japan" conference in Albuquerque, New Mexico. In his talk at the conference, MM explained how Japan combines tradition with practicality by demonstrating the Japanese tea ceremony. Explaining the Japanese respect for handicraft, MM showed what was supposedly an antique teacup. He poured in the tea and, following tea ceremony custom, carefully revolved the cup three times. Then, he proceeded to eat the cup. Though appearing to be a proper ceramic teacup, it was made of edible flour paste. To his friend's delight, MM slyly counteracted the stereotype of the humorless Japanese. He showed there is often more than what is seen.

Now, MM, Japan's most famous simultaneous interpreter who started the first Japanese school of simultaneous interpretation, the man who enabled governments to communicate more efficiently and clearly with each other, my friend who helped guide me during my initial explorations of a very foreign culture, can no longer speak.

I feel an unfamiliar sadness—unfamiliar because I rarely, if ever, feel sadness about disability, my own or someone else's. Having been born disabled, I usually associate disability with adaptation, not with loss. To me, thus far, disability has not been about loss. It has been about the body's mutability, about time.

Is my sadness about MM's loss? Or is what I feel more about my loss, not having him at my side as I continue to experience Japan?

Or is what I feel related to how I now see my life as having a before and an after?

There is no doubt that MM's stroke has left him unable to live the life he was accustomed to living. But still I question: is it MM's impairment that leads to loss or is it the inability to imagine a different life for him that is more the cause?

I want to help others imagine different lives than what is prescribed. I want my research to provide a deeper understanding of disability in Japan, to communicate the rich disability history that too often cannot be seen in Japanese culture. Like Lafcadio Hearn did with tales of old Japan, can I popularize old Japanese tales that incorporate disability? In this way, can I give back to the culture at least some of what Japan has given to me?

I accept a Fulbright Commission invitation to present my research. I start reading Tanizaki Jun'ichirō, one of the most famous Japanese writers of the twentieth century, because I have yet to come across anyone who looks at Tanizaki's notable characters with disabilities.

A few weeks later, I want to tell MM what I've been discovering. I contact the woman who arranges visits for MM. She surprises me by saying that MM's friends can no longer visit him. MM has had another stroke. His wife refuses all visitors.

I think of how the Japanese often keep disability and serious illness, still a sign of shame, from public view. But then, the woman continues: "I think his wife is getting back at him for all of his dalliances with women." This confession makes me laugh. Not only do I remember all the younger women, mostly former students, to whom MM introduced me. What she tells me also corresponds to what I know of the Japanese vendetta, the Japanese idea of revenge.

I once again think of how much importance Fukushima-sensei placed on communication. Hidden away by his wife, MM will no longer be able to communicate his unique understanding of humor, of his culture, of the joy he felt for the world.

That night I read about Yamamoto Kansuke.

During the great Japanese civil wars, the Shingen Takeda family employed Yamamoto, a military general once widely known in Japan. He was ugly, blind in one eye, and had a crippled leg and no fingers. His body was full of scars. Yamamoto's shrewd military tactics and ability to analyze information was legendary; he could visualize detailed geography, the shape of a castle, the situation of the castle town, and movements of people as if all of this was happening right in front of him. He was able to create a three-dimensional world based on what he gleaned from books and stories.

However, the official books by the Takeda family do not mention Yamamoto Kansuke. Nor does any book by the family's vassals. He is no longer depicted as the brilliant military general he actually was.

I wonder what MM would make of this: in Japanese history, as society moved from an imperial society to a warrior society, those deemed physically different disappear.

Four

|||||||

Rare and Uncommon Beings

My winter T-cell result is alarming: 122.

The cause might be my immune system's reaction to the hepatitis and flu vaccines, which could cause a drop of T cells. Or it might be a more permanent decline. We do not know. With my T cells so low, Dr. Shay tells me I need to go on Bactrim to prevent pneumocystis, the rare pneumonia that killed many of the first people diagnosed with AIDS.

Dr. Shay also says it is time to think about starting the "cocktail" of antiretroviral medications. I have wanted to avoid this during my time in Japan. I don't want the high toxicity of the drugs and their disturbing side effects to interfere with my life here. And there's the practical issue: how will I get the drugs here in Japan?

Bactrim is easily prescribed at the medical clinic and easily paid for. But the very expensive antiretroviral drugs are another story.

I'm also afraid to begin taking the medications when I'm alone. I ask Dr. Shay if I can wait until Ian arrives late next month.

"You can probably wait that long," Dr. Shay replies.

I can use the health insurance I've kept in the U.S. Dr. Shay can prescribe a month's supply. Reiko in New York City will pick up and fill the prescription. Then, she will mail the drugs to Ian in DC. My insurance drug plan also allows me to mail order by phone a three-month's supply that can be sent directly to Ian. He will bring all the drugs with him. I will then have a four-month supply.

Putting aside the chance that my body's reaction to the initial medications might warrant a quick change to other medications, I tell Dr. Shay my plan. Dr. Shay gives his okay. I put the plan into action. Once all the details are set, I go to the medical clinic to pick up and fill the Bactrim prescription.

Returning to my room, even though I'm exhausted, my anxiety keeps me from resting. I frantically research online to learn everything I can about the antiretroviral drugs. I do not like what I find.

I spend the entire night online trying to predict every possible outcome. At 11:00 p.m., I get my nightly text message from Mike: "Are you home?"

Immediately, I call him.

"What's wrong?" he asks. Even though he has not known me very long, he already knows from the sound of my voice when I'm not doing well.

"I don't want to tell you," I say, barely able to speak. All of a sudden, all my anxiety, so familiar from the beginning of other relationships, has risen in my stomach, my chest, and my throat. My head is pounding. I'm having difficulty breathing.

"Take it slow. There's no need to have a panic attack." I can't remember telling Mike about my panic attacks. Maybe he's read about it in my memoir, which I gave him over Christmas?

"T cells," I'm finally able to say. "They're low. Down to 122."

"You'll need more than low T cells to get rid of me."

I'm stunned. How is Mike able to know what to say when I need it said?

I try as hard as I can, but I can't respond. It seems way too early in our relationship to risk saying to him what I most want to say.

"That's okay," Mike says. "I love you, too."

I sit on my single bed in my small room in Tokyo, holding my cell phone to my ear. I start to heave before I realize I am crying.

"It's going to be a long four weeks until I see you again," I tell this man who holds his cell phone to his ear in a room I've never seen over five hundred miles away on a different island in northern Japan.

"Next time, don't wait until I'm home to let me know what's going on."

I start the Bactrim.

Two days later I develop a fever. I remember Dr. Shay told me to watch for unexplained fever. I also feel a lump in my neck, which I assume to be a swollen lymph node: another sign Dr. Shay told me to watch for.

I go to the medical clinic to see the doctor. He checks my throat and sees no sign of an infection to explain both the fever and the swollen lymph node.

"If the fever persists, there's not much else I can do for you," he tells me. "We'd have to put you in the hospital, and I don't have any hospital privileges. With your having HIV, hospitals here won't treat you. There's one hospital that deals with patients with HIV, but I don't think you'd want to go there."

Back in my room, I convince myself I have lymphoma. I just read in the paper that a well-known middle-aged playwright in New York City died of lymphoma. Those lymph nodes in my lung, the ones that initially alerted Dr. Shay that something was awry, must be spreading throughout my body. I've been back from the doctor less than an hour and already I've worked myself into a panic. I can't get lymphoma—dying from lymphoma—out of my mind.

Later that night, when I talk to Mike, I do not tell him any of this. I just tell him I'm tired and need to go to sleep. I figure if the fever and swollen gland persist, I can always tell him later.

The next day I sleep until noon. I take my temperature. It's normal. The swollen lymph node in my neck seems to be gone, as well.

I send an e-mail to Dr. Shay.

"Could have been a reaction to the Bactrim," he responds.

Before the T-cell drop, before starting on Bactrim, before the fever and lymph node scare, there didn't seem to be a reason to tell my Japanese friends what was going on. Now, it seems it's time to tell Mika.

I meet Mika for lunch at an Edo-period soba shop. After we eat, I say, "There's something I need to tell you."

Mika's eyes perk up a bit as she waits for me to tell her.

"I've yet to tell you that right before I returned to Japan, I tested positive for HIV."

I pause, not knowing if there's anything else I need to say. So far, there's little reaction. What reaction did I expect? Surely, Mika, being properly Japanese, wouldn't get up and leave me alone at the table.

"I'm scared," I hear myself say.

Mika looks directly at me. "Is there anything you need me to do for you right now?" The pent-up anxiety escapes from my body in one long breath. At this table in this old soba shop, nothing has actually changed. But now, with the information I've been holding within me for months now known to one more person, everything seems changed.

"I haven't been sleeping well. And I've been having panic attacks. Maybe you can take me to your healer?"

"Sure. I'm going to see him on Thursday if you'd like to come along. I'll translate what you want me to tell him into Japanese."

Mika has been going to Mogi-sensei, her healer, ever since she developed problems singing because of her teeth and jaw. When a doctor and a dentist couldn't explain what was going on, Mika went to Mogi-sensei. Having had many negative experiences with Western medicine as a child, I've often resorted to acupuncture, homeopathy, and other kinds of "alternative" treatment. Nothing to lose. Anything is worth a try. A visit to Mogi-sensei only costs 4,000 yen, about forty dollars.

On the way to Mogi-sensei, I ask Mika what he actually does.

"He works with the energy he sees from your body," she says. "It is difficult to explain."

Mogi-sensei does not take appointments. We take off our shoes in the office *genkan*. Mika introduces me to one of Mogi-sensei's assistants, who, dressed all in white, looks like a nurse.

We sit with about a half-dozen others, mostly elderly women, in the waiting room. From beyond a thin wall, I hear a man talking. I assume he is Mogi-sensei. Every so often the nurse calls out a name, and someone from the waiting room gets up and walks beyond the wall. After one person enters to see Mogi-sensei, another exits, puts on her shoes, and leaves.

After about a half-hour wait, the nurse calls, "Mika-san. Kenny-san."

"That's us," I say, as if Mika wouldn't know.

We go beyond the wall. I watch what Mika does: She hangs up her coat, so I hang up my coat. She empties her pockets of money and all metal objects, so I do the same. She sits on a short stool; I sit next to her on another short stool.

We watch Mogi-sensei treat a middle-aged man who sits on the edge of a familiar doctor's examination table.

I'm surprised by the lack of privacy. Mogi-sensei stands nearby with his back to us. Across the room is the man he is treating. The man speaks Japanese words I do not understand. Every so often, Mogi-sensei says something that sounds like "whoosh."

The man, following what I assume are Mogi-sensei's instructions, gets up and goes over to another table. This table also looks like a doctor's examination table. But this table is vertical, perpendicular to the floor. The man grabs onto handholds on each side of the table. Mogi-sensei presses a button and the table moves until it is parallel to the floor. He deftly places a single acupuncture needle in the man's head. He manipulates the man's legs a bit. He removes the acupuncture needle. Then, he presses the button again. The table returns to its vertical position.

The man returns to sit on the edge of the first examination table; Mogi-sensei moves back to where he previously stood. The man gets up and does some golfing motions. He nods his head a few times, each time more vigorously. I guess the man was having a problem with his shoulder. This impaired his golf game. Whatever Mogi-sensei has done seems to have relieved the man. He leaves the room happy.

Now, it's my turn. As I move to the examination table, the white-clad assistant offers me a plastic tray in which I put my glasses.

Mika talks to Mogi-sensei. Mogi-sensei nods his head as Mika tells him what I want him to know.

"He's never had a patient with HIV before," she translates. "But that is not a problem."

Not a problem for him, I think.

Mogi-sensei stands across the room, like he did with the golfer who just departed. Although he's looking at me, he seems to be looking through me, or actually just to the right of me. After a "whoosh," he says something to Mika.

"He says you're wearing a metal chain and that's no good. It doesn't allow your body's energy to flow freely."

He's right. I do wear a metal chain, on which hangs my Coumadin medical alert tag, around my neck. I'll have to get a nonmetal chain. I remove the chain and set it in the same plastic tray as my glasses.

Mogi-sensei approaches me. He lifts up my right shoulder a few times. Each time, he says something to the assistant. She writes what he says in my file. He motions for me to put my right thumb and forefinger together. He pulls the fingers apart. Once again, he says something to the assistant. She writes it down.

It is time for me to go to the vertical table. I hold on to the handholds as the table moves. My blood rushes to my head. Face down into the table, I'm having trouble breathing. Mogi-sensei briefly whisks an acupuncture needle into the top of my head. He moves my legs up and down. If he knew English, or if I knew Japanese, I'd tell him I don't have calves, like I did in the New York City hospital. But even if we did speak the same language, I'm not sure he'd understand.

I'm back on the other table. Mogi-sensei is looking at me in his slightly askance way. What does he see?

As if answering my question, Mika translates: "He says he sees much of the virus on the right side of your body and in your lungs. But this is nothing to worry about."

Easy for him to say.

"He says you should feel less tired and have more energy soon."

I nod my head, hoping this is true.

After Mika's treatment, we pay the white-clad attendant. Back in the street, I thank Mika for taking me to Mogi-sensei.

Eating an early dinner, Mika reminds me, "You can't take a bath for twenty-four hours, but a shower is okay."

That night, in my room, I am able to concentrate on my research for the first time in weeks. I have no idea what it was that Mogi-sensei did. But just like I gratefully accept Japan itself, even though there's so much I might never understand, the effect of his treatment is just what I need. After talking with Mike, I sleep through the night for the first time since I've returned to Japan.

I'm woken up by a loud knock on the metal door.

It's a mailman delivering a package. I wasn't expecting a package. I look to see who it's from, but the return address is in Japanese.

I open the package. It's a Daruma, the hollow, round, legless, armless, and eyeless doll who has sacred power.

I've been told that a Daruma with eyes is bad luck. Once given eyes, Daruma loses his power and must be given peace and rest. When we dispose of him, he will sleep forever. Daruma is yet another stereotypical depiction of a blind man as seer, someone with sacred powers. When his sight is restored, he becomes powerless.

One of Matsui-sensei's PhD students first told me about Daruma. She knows of my quest to gather as much as I can about disability representation in Japanese culture for my upcoming presentation at the Fulbright Commission. She must have sent this Daruma to me.

Now fully awake, I spend the day preparing my presentation.

I read Hanada-sensei's long list of *marebito*, rare and uncommon beings, in Japanese legend.

The phone rings.

T cells: 231.

I e-mail Dr. Shay. In his reply, he says this is a good sign; the decline in my T cells was most likely due to the vaccines. Now that my T cells are back over 200, I can stop taking the Bactrim. But he still thinks I should stick to the plan and start the antiretrovirals when Ian arrives.

Five

||||||||

Bubbling Water

I was twelve when I stayed up late every night to watch the Sapporo Winter Olympics on television. I watched the ABC broadcast until the last credits rolled. After John Denver sang the "Yokoso Sapporo" song, I finally allowed myself to sleep. Now, decades later, I am on my way to see Mike for Yuki Matsuri. At Sapporo's Chitose Airport, there are "Yokoso Japan" signs, part of a new tourist ad campaign to welcome visitors.

I meet Toni, Mike's Australian co-teacher and friend at Sapporo Station. It is Saturday and Mike is working; Toni is on a more typical weekends-off teaching schedule. She has Mike's keys. After lunch she'll escort me to Mike's apartment.

Once again all my insecurities rise to the surface. For some reason I've convinced myself that Mike doesn't really want me to visit him in Sapporo. If actual facts might combat my insecurity, what Toni is telling me over lunch should put to rest my ridiculous anxiety.

"He talks about you all the time. Kenny this, Kenny that. At school, when we go out for drinks after work," she says in her thick Australian accent. "I've been here for five years and I can't find myself a man."

What I first notice about the Sapporo streets are the piles of packed snow on which we're walking. When we turn left at the first corner, then right down a smaller street, the piles of snow get increasingly higher. We stop in front of what I assume is Mike's building—Sunshine Shiroishi (why are so many buildings in Japan named Sunshine?). A narrow path chiseled out of two densely packed piles of snow leads into the building.

I thank Toni for meeting me with Mike's keys and showing me the way to his apartment. "My pleasure, darling," she says. "I'll see you soon."

Mike's apartment is big by Japanese standards, especially in comparison to my Tokyo room. Along the entrance hallway is a laundry room with a sink, which leads into the shower and bath. At the end of the hallway, to the left is a well-stocked kitchen with many pots and pans hanging on the wall, and a full-sized refrigerator, much bigger than my not-even-waist-high Tokyo refrigerator.

To the right the apartment opens up into a living room. I peek out onto the small snow-packed terrace. I remember Mike telling me that he keeps the heat on only in his bedroom; in the living room he uses a traditional *kotatsu*, a heater placed underneath the low table surrounded by a few cushioned floor chairs.

I open the sliding door to Mike's bedroom. Mike's bed is filled with plush Tiggers. He hasn't told me about this. I smile. I rest among the Tiggers on Mike's bed, where I imagine he has talked with me on his cell phone every night since we first met. I breathe in Mike's by-now-familiar smell.

I meet Mike after work. We head to Susukino, the lively Sapporo nightlife district. We go to a noodle shop and order a Sapporo specialty: *bata-kan ramen*.

We look down at our steaming-hot bowls of noodles. On top of the delectably looking noodles is yellow corn and just-as-yellow butter.

"Butter corn," we both say at the same time, enjoying the Japanese attempt at the replication of English words.

After eating, we zip up our winter jackets and go to see this year's Yuki Matsuri. Blocks and blocks of the city park are filled with a variety of ice and snow sculptures. The sculptures range from my height to arena-size, from famous celebrities to animals real and imagined. I'm delighted to see Pikachu, my totem Pokémon, as well as Winnie-the-Pooh and his friends from the Christopher Robin forest.

"I guess you've met the Tiggers." Mike smiles his slightly goofy smile.

We watch the small children play in the ice maze and rush down the ice slides. I think about the enormous effort made at creating these enjoyable ice objects, which, after a few weeks, will be hauled away. Are they allowed to dissolve naturally or are they destroyed?

Our time together in Sapporo is filled with a perfect mixture of fun, both in and out of bed. We go out with Mike's boisterous friends. Watching them unwind after a week of teaching reminds me not only of my first stay in Japan but also that Mike and his friends are fifteen or more years younger than I am.

Though I'm still waiting for the result of my last T-cell test, my worries about my health mostly stay in the background. Mike makes sure I remember to take my nightly dose of Coumadin. I acknowledge my anxiety about starting the antiretrovirals when Ian brings them.

During our conversations, Mike and I take our first tentative steps toward talking about the future. We talk about the possibility of my staying on and teaching in Tokyo after my Fulbright; Mike talks of asking for a transfer to teach in Tokyo so we can be together. We talk about how best to use Mike's remaining vacation days so we can see each other as much as possible during the coming months. Mike plans to accompany me on a trip to Tōno, home of much Japanese folklore.

We go to the oddly named Daruma to eat *jinguskan* (pronounced Genghis Khan). This Sapporo tradition is flame-grilled lamb. We know we've found the right place when we see the red lantern and the grimacing, bald Genghis Khan, as well as a sizable line outside.

Once inside, my glasses immediately fog up. Clearing my glasses reveals a very cozy, as in very small, very friendly, very old place. There are about twenty-five stools around a three-sided counter. Behind the counter are three elderly women with bandanas tied around their heads. It looks as if the women are as old as the mutton grime; decades and decades of barbecue stain the walls. As we devour the lamb, Mike and I keep nodding to each other with each bite, agreeing that this food is absolutely delicious.

After our feast we head to the building that houses all of Sapporo's gay bars. The bar Mike takes me to is only slightly larger than my room in Tokyo.

No sooner have we sat down at the bar than the bartender says, "*Jinguskan tabe mashita ka?*"

Even I understand what the bartender has asked. He wants to know if we enjoyed the *jinguskan* we just ate. We're both embarrassed as we realize our clothes smell like the walls of Daruma.

For Valentine's Day we go to Noboribetsu to stay at an *onsen* with thirty different baths overlooking a steaming lunar-like landscape created by an ancient volcanic eruption.

After the hour-and-a-half train ride, we walk up the small main street of the town. It begins to snow. I run a bit ahead, and when I turn around, it seems as if Mike, carrying our two-days' worth of luggage against the wind, is in the midst of one of the famous *ukiyo-e* woodblock prints of a snowy day on the Tōkaidō highway.

The woman who takes us to our room says something about the *yukata*. She takes one of the *yukata* neatly folded on the low table with her. Very quickly she returns. She displays another *yukata* she has brought with her.

"*Ah, arigato gozaimashita,*" I say, bowing slightly. I thank her for realizing the *yukata* in the room would be too long for me. The new one is smaller and should fit me better. I tell Mike about the elderly Japanese woman who, at the *onsen* almost three and a half years ago, taught me to adapt the *yukata* so I wouldn't trip or accidentally expose myself naked to passersby.

Mike is delighted at our tatami-matted room. His apartment is Western style. He has never stayed in a tatami-matted room before.

Over the course of the afternoon, we try all thirty baths. There is an outdoor *rotemburo*, which becomes Mike's favorite. Sitting in the indescribably hot bath in the well-below-freezing outdoors is something neither of us have yet experienced. Icicles form on the small washcloth-like white towel that is traditionally placed on one's head when bathing at an *onsen*.

A group of young boys runs in and out of the hot water into the snow piled on the side of the bath. The boys bring snow back with them into the bath. The snow immediately melts in the scalding water.

Back inside, I enter a tepid circular bath filled with constantly replenishing bubbles. "I must find out what's in the water that does this," I tell Mike. "It feels as if I'm in a Doris Day movie."

"You look like you're on one of those crazy Japanese game shows." Mike provides what is perhaps a more precise description: the inane TV programs in which bizarre and brightly costumed contestants are forced to run through all kinds of ridiculous obstacles on a prefab set designed in 1970s retro style.

All I know is that I can't remember laughing so much or being so happy as I am now with Mike. He watches me as he sits beneath a waterfall of hot water. That's the bath that awaits me as soon as I'm finished frolicking in the Doris Day bath filled with effervescent, endless bubbles.

Just a few years ago, I wouldn't have been able to enjoy the time as much as I have the past week. I would have let the gnawing uncertainty about my health override everything else. Is this because of Mike? Or because I'm now older? Is it because of Japan?

Years ago, at the start of yet another relationship with a man who lived in a different place than I did, I began to be concerned that this was somehow a bad pattern that I created for myself.

As I told this to a friend, he laughed.

"Why are you laughing?" I asked.

"You travel all the time and are rarely home. Of course you're going to meet men who live in places you don't live."

So, it wasn't a bad thing after all. Still, it made the relationships, especially at the beginning, with all the comings and goings, all the reunions and good-byes, more difficult, more fraught.

Now, returning to Tokyo, I think about what is ahead for me. Will any of this ever get any easier over time?

I read "A Portrait of Shunkin," Tanizaki's famous story about a samisen player who becomes blind as a young girl. Shunkin has an often-tortured relationship with Sasuke, her merchant family's apprentice. Despite Shunkin's cruel treatment of Sasuke, the two become secret lovers.

The story, and their relationship, takes a dramatic turn. While Shunkin sleeps, someone—we do not know who (is it Sasuke himself?)—throws boiling water at her face. Her face is badly scarred. Shunkin does not want anyone to see her.

Sasuke blinds himself, not only so Shunkin will allow him to be with her but also to remember Shunkin always as the beautiful woman he knew. He preserves his "imperishable ideal" of her beauty: Shunkin's exquisite white face, "as it had looked until only two months ago." Her face "hovered before him in a circle of dim light, like the radiant halo of the Buddha."

Is this the Japanese antithesis to *mono no aware*, an attempt, however fruitless, to freeze a moment in time, to halt time itself, to keep beauty, and our love of beauty—and love itself?—from slipping away?

That night Mike sends me a text message a bit earlier than usual. The message tells me to call him as soon as possible. As soon as I'm back in my room, I call.

"My father died."

"You're kidding."

"He died in the morning of a heart attack. I'm trying to get a ticket back home tomorrow or the day after."

"How long will you be gone?"

"I don't know. Probably three weeks. I have to use my remaining vacation time. I won't be able to travel with you to Tōno next month."

"Don't worry about that. I wish I could go back to Canada with you."

"I know you can't do that. You have your health stuff to deal with and Ian is coming over."

"If you're flying through Narita, I can meet you if you have time between planes. How are you?"

"After crying in the shower for an hour, I've been playing computer games all night."

"I wish I was with you."

"Just having you to talk to helps."

When we get off the phone, I feel useless. But he's right. With my needing to start the antiretrovirals, which Ian will bring with him next week, there's no way I can accompany him back to Canada.

Somehow, while being separated over five thousand miles by continents and oceans, I'm going to have to find a way to support Mike through this at the same time as dealing with whatever the medications might throw my way.

That night I call Mike again before I go to sleep. And I call him the next morning, and in the afternoon. We talk again that night, and the next day I meet him for a quick lunch during his layover at Narita.

"I love you," I say just before he has to go to the departure gate.

"I love you, too," he says before disappearing beyond the security check and immigration doors.

As I stare at the closed door, I know if it wasn't for my health I would be on the other side of those doors. I would be going to Canada with him.

Alone on my way back from the airport, I panic. As irrational as the thought may be, I feel as if, somehow, I have brought death unexpectedly into Mike's life.

Six

My Japan

Two days after Mike departs for Canada, I am back at Narita Airport to welcome Ian to Japan.

When we get back to my room, Ian gives me the four-month supply of antiretrovirals. I store them safely in my desk drawer. I do not want to deal with side effects while showing Japan to Ian. I do not want to be alone the first day after taking the medication. The plan is to start taking the pills three nights before Ian's departure.

During Ian's visit, I get up every night in the middle of the night to call Mike and see how he's doing in Canada. Unlike my first stay in Japan, this time I have lived firmly in one time zone. Now, with Mike in Canada, I am once again aware of what time it is back in North America. On the day of Mike's father's funeral, I calculate the right time to send him flowers.

Ian and I travel to Kyoto. I show him my favorite gardens that have taught me so much about Japan.

We go to Joko no Niwa, the prehistoric garden at Matsuo Taisha, a modern rendering of *iwakura*, a group of large sacred rocks that is home to *kami*. As the garden moves up the hill, the rocks get larger, weighing up to eight tons. The design of the rocks is such that at the highest point of the hill, the largest, heaviest rock seems to defy gravity. At any moment it is poised to fly away—or come crashing down the hill.

Ian wants to see a geisha.

So, one rainy night, we go to Gion. We walk down a street lined by *machiya*, the old Kyoto wooden houses, and red lanterns. We hear a car stop beyond us. We turn around and see a taxi driver getting out of his taxi. By the time he reaches the other side of the taxi, he has opened a large umbrella. He opens the passenger side door, and a geisha, in full geisha regalia, emerges. As the umbrella-wielding taxi driver escorts her into one of the wooden *machiya*, her wooden *geta* echo on the wet pavement.

Our last night in Kyoto, we stay at a *ryokan*. Dressed in our *yukata*, Ian and I sit on cushions on either side of the low lacquer table. A kneeling kimono-clad young woman serves the first course; the second course is served by another. After yet another kimono-clad young woman serves us our third course, Ian asks, "Will each course be served by a different woman?"

As if in answer, the shoji slides open and the same kimono-clad young woman who served our first course enters to serve the fourth course.

Over three hours later, after we have finished our nine or more courses—I always lose count of how many courses are served during *kaiseki*, even though each time I vow to count and remember—Ian has been transported to that place I've experienced so many times in Japan.

"I can't believe it's just as you described it to me," he tells me, finally admitting that I have not "romanticized" Japan.

It is time for his bath. I tell him it's usual to immerse yourself in the extremely hot water for about twenty minutes.

While Ian is in the bath, I call Mike. "How are you?"

"It feels as if I've been punched in the stomach. When I get up in the morning, it feels as if it's all been a dream."

"That's how I've felt ever since I've known about the virus."

After he tells me about the funeral, he asks, "Are you ready to start taking the meds?"

"When we're back in Tokyo."

"Shouldn't Ian be back from the bath by now?"

Over an hour later, Ian returns to our room.

"Where were you?"

"It was amazing. I just couldn't get out of the tub."

"It's a good thing there seems to be only one other occupied room in the *ryokan*."

We laugh, and the more we try to quiet our laughter, the more we can't stop laughing.

I now have two more days before starting my medication, and my time with Ian is beginning to feel like a version of a newly inducted soldier's last night on the town. These are the last days of my life that I won't be tethered to taking the medications that can save my life.

The morning we leave Kyoto, I get up early. Once again, I drink the healing waters from the Otawa waterfall at Kiyomizudera.

On our way back to Tokyo, we stop at Atami to see the famous *White and Red Plum Blossoms* screen by Kōrin, my favorite Japanese artist.

In Atami I realize that it is about time for the actual plum blossoms to be in bloom. Before heading to the museum, we stop at the tourist office.

"Are there plum blossoms?" I ask the English-speaking tourist office worker.

"I don't think so."

"If there were plum blossoms, where might they be?"

"Mmmmm. I'm not sure. But maybe at the Baien."

After she shows me on the map where the Baien is in relation to the museum, we're on our way to see the Kōrin screen.

The Kōrin screen is actually two screens, each just over five feet wide and five and a half feet high. The moment Ian sees the screens, he puts his right hand over his mouth, which I know means he is overwhelmed.

Flowing up the center, curves and circles crystallize in the ripples on the brown surface of the dark stream—critics have yet to discover the secret of how Kōrin has seemingly cut the brown lines out of the bluish-silver ground. The carefully observed plum trees—white blossoms on the left, red blossoms on the right—contrast with the abstraction of the design. The blossoms themselves are echoed in the silvery-green patches of moss on the trunks of the plum trees.

After sitting silently in front of the screen for what could be ten minutes or an hour, we leave the museum and take a taxi to the Baien. As we get closer to the Baien, the traffic thickens. We see groups and groups of people walking the same way we are going.

Released from the taxi, I am running through the crowd. In front of me, I see plum tree after plum tree—all in blossom: white, light pink, dark pink, and every shade of red—flowing up two sides of a small stream. Amid the crowd of mostly elderly Japanese couples enjoying a sun-drenched late winter afternoon, I cannot control my tears.

One night Mike was talking to his father; the next day his father was dead. I don't want to get sick. I don't want to die. There is still so much to see, so much I want to do.

I turn around to find Ian. He is right behind me, taking photo after photo of the plum trees. He takes photo after photo of me as I run among the profusion of blossoms.

Ian knows what I'm feeling. I don't have to explain any of it to him.

Our first night back in Tokyo, the night I plan to start taking the medications, we stay out too late. I postpone.

I call Mike.

"We came home too late for me to start the meds tonight."

"You're going to have to do it."

"I know. I just want to do it right. Whatever that means."

Ian is leaving on Saturday morning, so I know that if I don't want to be alone the first day on the meds, I will have to start taking the medications tomorrow night.

The next night I make sure we get home early. At eleven o'clock I enter what I see as the beginning of the rest of my life: I take the two pills—one yellow, one blue—that contain the cocktail of three medications that hopefully will keep the virus at bay so my immune system can remain functional.

In the middle of the night, I wake up feeling both euphoric and extremely dizzy. It is as if I am high in a funhouse, but it is actually not much fun. The small room expands and contracts with no certain pattern. Unable to tell what is going to happen moment to moment, I am unsettled as much by uncertainty as I am by the ever-shifting room.

I wake up Ian to make sure he knows what is going on. My voice seems to echo, oddly. At first, it speeds up. Then, it slows down.

No one warned me about this. It feels as if I get out of bed, I could fly, which is decidedly not something that should be felt in the middle of the night in a small room in Tokyo or anywhere else.

I am able to fall back asleep, if it could be called sleep. My dreams are in vivid three dimensions. Everyone in the dream has voices that echo like my voice when I woke up Ian earlier in the night.

In the morning I can't remember who or what I dreamed of, but I know I am still extremely dizzy. I can barely keep my head up.

But this is Ian's last day in Tokyo. I am determined that we do not spend his last day in my small room. We have reserved tickets at the new Ghibli Museum, devoted to the anime of Miyazaki. The museum is in Mitaka, a suburb west of Tokyo.

Ian thinks I'm crazy.

I tell him I want to monitor what it is going to be like on the meds out in the world with someone I trust. I figure this will be a good test so

I'll know what I might expect in the days ahead if the side effects persist. "The worst thing that can happen is I get sick and we need to take a taxi home."

Getting ready to go, my nausea increases. On the way to the subway, I need to stop to get my bearings. When we change trains, I'm thankful there are bathrooms in Japanese train stations. I make it just in time to vomit.

On the train to Mitaka, I can't lift my head to see where we are. I tell Ian where we need to get off so he can make sure we don't miss our stop.

By the time we get to the station, the dizziness has started to pass. I feel somewhat myself again, though an imbalanced version of myself. I feel strong enough to walk to the museum instead of taking a taxi.

We walk along the narrow Tamagawa. Here, in 1948, the writer Dazai Osamu, then thirty-nine, and his mistress drowned: a double suicide. Now, the river is so shallow. Total immersion in its water would be impossible, let alone dangerous.

At the museum, I take it slow. I am hungry and thirsty but afraid eating will bring back the nausea.

At the museum's outdoor café, Ian convinces me I can have some of the homemade apple ices. I slowly taste the sweet yet sour ices. I'm feeling well enough to try to eat some food.

Ian seems exhausted. Last night and today has taken a lot out of both of us.

"I'm glad we went to the museum today," I say.

"You're the only one I know who can start off the day like you did and end up in better shape than I am."

The next morning I walk Ian down the hill to the bus that will take him to the airport.

"Thank you so much," I say as I hug him good-bye. "I hope you had a good time."

"I had a great time. I now know your Japan firsthand. Take care of yourself."

I watch Ian board the bus. I watch the bus as it disappears down the busy Tokyo street.

As I walk back up the hill to my room, I'm sure Ian and I now have the relationship that's best for both of us. It took my return to Japan and meeting Mike to accept this fully. Ian knows me as well as anyone. He has seen how happy I am here, despite the difficulties that have been thrown my way. And now, Ian knows, firsthand, my Japan.

Back in my room, total exhaustion hits me. But I'm glad that I soldiered on against the physical odds yesterday. At least now I am familiar with what it might be like living with the side effects of the medications.

Are *kami*, present in mountains, trees, waterfalls, rocks, as well as in manmade objects, also present in the pills?

The possible presence of *kami* notwithstanding, I'm not looking forward to taking the meds tonight. I'd rather not have to go through even a semblance of what I've gone through since taking the pills two nights ago. But I take them in the hope they will stop the decline of my immune system. There is danger in missing even one dose. The virus mutates very easily and then becomes resistant to the drugs.

I once again think of all the therapists and all my friends who insisted I was strong enough to deal with whatever came my way. Now, as much as I resist, I'm learning that perhaps they were right. I cannot believe how much I've been dealing with the past six months, especially these past weeks. But still I'm so happy to be in Japan.

The phone rings, and I don't know where I am. I must have fallen asleep on the floor.

It's Mike calling from Canada, checking in to see how I am doing with the meds. We admit we're both exhausted. On Wednesday, Mike will return. I will meet him at Narita and accompany him on the one-and-a-half-hour bus ride to Haneda, where he will catch his plane to Sapporo.

Although Mike has sounded okay on the phone the past three weeks, I wonder what will be the effect of his father's death. With all we have been through in such a short time, what will it be like to see him again?

I am still nauseous from the drugs. I've not been out of my apartment since Ian left on Saturday morning. Leaving the safety of my room, I discover I am still dizzy, unbalanced, when I go outside into the clear springlike day.

To get my bearings, I first go to Koishikawa Kōrakuen, an early seventeenth-century stroll garden, which is close to where I can catch the train to Narita. Winding my way through the garden's paths, I pass ponds, stone lanterns, and waterfalls. When I cross the lake over the humped Full Moon Bridge, I see how the bridge completes itself in its watered reflection.

I make my way to the garden's northeast corner to see what I have come to see: the plum trees still in late blossom. Even from a distance, I can see the white, pink, and red blossoms. This brings back some of the ecstasy I felt when first seeing the plum blossoms in Atami, the day before I started taking the pills. The cheerfully colored flowers, the gnarled trunks and branches, and the fragrance in the air as I approach seem to be the perfect antidote for the side effects caused by the medications.

If only such a natural phenomenon as what I see before me could keep the virus itself at bay. But too soon—it is already past the middle of March—these blossoms will be gone, not only from the trees but also from the ground where so many have fallen.

Soon after—exactly when, we never quite know—there will be different blossoms, the traditional sakura, the celebrated cherry blossoms for which Japan is most known. Perhaps there might not be a distinct separation between before taking the pills and after.

I wait for Mike in the international arrivals area. When I first met him at the airport in November, I had no idea I would now be waiting for him to return from his father's funeral.

The door to the customs and baggage claim area opens. A straggle of arriving passengers emerges carrying and pulling their luggage after them. And then there is Mike, dressed in the same greenish-gray suit as when I first saw him four months ago.

But now Mike looks haggard. Though he happily greets me, it is not with the same nervous expectation of our first meeting. How could it be? Grief is a long process. I know I want to be with Mike through all of it, just as he has been there with me, supporting me through all I've gone through since we met.

On the bus to Haneda, our transformed bodies still remember each other. His hand easily fits into mine. His head rests gently on my shoulder.

Leaving the intimacy of the bus behind, our time together is much too short. Mike's plane is scheduled to leave within the hour.

Outside the terminal the dizziness returns. I can hardly look up.

"There's no need for you to come inside," Mike says. Does he sense that my body is ready to expire?

"Are you sure?"

"I'll call you when I get in."

"I'll see you soon in Sapporo."

We hug. Mike enters the terminal doors.

Waiting outside for my bus to arrive, I feel I might never see Mike again. After his father's death, he can't be the same. After I started taking the pills, I am different. Once again, despite all I've learned, as if it were possible, I want to turn back time.

Seven

Before and After

I arrange to interview two of the surviving *genbaku otome*, the so-called Hiroshima Maidens. Before returning to Hiroshima, I learn as much as I can about the twenty-five *hibakusha* who traveled from Japan to the United States for medical treatment in May 1955.

The Hiroshima Maidens project began with meetings of young female *hibakusha* at the Reverend Tanimoto Kiyoshi's Nagarekawa Church. The group's main goal was to help the young women regain emotional stability through reading the Scripture. Though many in the group did not become practicing Christians, the group did offer some members medical treatment in Tokyo.

Norman Cousins, the pacifist editor of the *Saturday Review*, visited Hiroshima in August 1953. Reverend Tanimoto introduced him to the group. Cousins asked Tanimoto what could be done to help the young women. A year and a half later, Cousins invited the group to the United States.

From the beginning, the U.S. government was unwilling to cooperate with the project. The government argued that treating the young women amounted to admitting U.S. culpability in dropping the atomic bomb, creating new obligations toward other *hibakusha*. Cousins was left to raise private money to bring the young women to the United States for medical treatment. With the help of Dr. William Hitzig, a family friend and the director of New York's Mount Sinai Hospital, he persuaded the Mount Sinai board of directors to agree to free surgery and hospitalization.

Packing for my trip to Hiroshima, I fixate on my pills. I think about earthquakes. What if there's an earthquake in Tokyo while I'm away? What if my trip takes longer than planned? How many pills should I take with me? Is it safe to leave the rest behind? Having many months' supply, I decide to take what I need with me plus an extra week, leaving the rest in my desk drawer.

How will I do on the medications? Alone in Hiroshima, will the side effects impinge upon my trip? Can I still do a trip like this on my own?

It is late afternoon when I return to Hiroshima. After settling in at my hotel, I walk to Peace Park. As it was during my first visit, the park is empty at this time of the afternoon. At the skeletal A-bomb dome, I notice there are some beams holding up some parts of the ruined building. Did I notice these support structures during my previous visit? Has there been some construction since the last time I was here?

As twilight approaches I walk past the Children's Memorial. Once again I find brightly colored paper cranes strewn around the monument.

I go for an early dinner at the Okonomi Mura, a warehouse-like four-story building that houses dozens of small stalls serving *okonomiyaki*, Japanese pancakes with layers of cabbage, bean sprouts, meat, fish, and noodles. Settling in at my chosen stand, which I think is the same one I ate at during my last visit, I order the special *okonomiyaki*, which has squid and other layers of I don't know what added.

After ordering, I notice the young woman next to me uses a wheelchair. I am surprised because I have not seen a wheelchair user outside Tokyo before.

As I walk back to my hotel, I think how last time my kinship with Numata-san, and even with Keiko-san, the interpreter with a limp, was because we are physically disabled.

Now, on the night before meeting with one of the surviving Hiroshima Maidens, the stigma feels more internal, invisible but more palpable, moving through my body as the radiation moved through the bodies of those who survived. Through no fault of their own, their lives were changed in ways unknowable at the time and, for those who remain, still unforeseen.

Here, during my first night of my return to Hiroshima, I know the changes in my life are as strong as the virus that hides in my body.

During the night I feel an urgent need to go to the bathroom. I've been told that the drugs can cause all sorts of digestive problems, but so far I've been lucky. Not so now. When I'm done, I notice blood in the toilet. I have no idea whether the cause is too much blood thinner or the antiretrovirals. If this continues, I will have to cancel my interviews and return to Tokyo.

In the morning the urgency in my stomach returns. This time, there's no sign of blood. I guess I can go on, after all.

I am scheduled to interview Sato Michio, who has invited me to her home outside Hiroshima. In a tatami-matted room around a low table, I sit with interpreter Keiko. Sato-san serves us tea. I notice a large quilt prominently displayed on the wall.

We talk about male *hibakusha* and why more attention is given to female survivors.

"Everybody likes beautiful women. So, they concentrate on girls, not boys," Sato-san says in her quiet but determined voice. "Everybody loves beauty."

When she says this, I make a connection to Tanizaki's Shunkin. When Shunkin doesn't allow anyone to see her scarred face, Sasuke blinds himself so he can only see what he used to see: Shunkin's face before it was marred by scalding water.

As Sato-san tells me her story, I am struck how, once again, her story contains images similar to other *hibakusha* stories: How far she was from where the bomb exploded. The flash. The fires. And the water.

"I tried to run away farther. I drank water but that water was very dirty. One of the soldiers said never to drink that water because you are burning. I was burned on my face so I couldn't think. My face was so swollen. I couldn't see anything. I don't know when, I don't know where, I just lay down. I heard the sound of a cart, maybe a cart with two wheels to carry dead bodies. I heard two soldiers. 'There is a dead body.' One of them picked me. 'There are so many dead bodies so we can't carry this one.' So I was left there. And I think this is destiny."

Hearing Sato-san's words, I think how Dr. Shay called my hospitalization for blood clots in my lung a "life-saving admission." What might have happened if I returned to Japan not knowing I needed to monitor what was going on with my immune system?

"What was your life like after you came back to Japan?"

"I have to think." She pauses. "Before going to the United States, I was working. I sewed. I used a sewing machine. After coming back, I was working, life was just the same. But people who met me said, 'Oh, you became more beautiful.'"

"Do you feel your Hiroshima Maiden experience was very important or just another experience in your life?"

"Yes. To go to the United States and to have plastic surgery is the most important part of my history."

"When did you start quilting?"

"My bedding at the Quaker host family was a quilt." She shows us a quilt pattern sample. "One part of the pattern means fire, another means love," she explains.

At first, I don't know why Sato-san is showing this specific quilt pattern to us. Then, as she explains it, I realize she is showing us a pattern from the quilt from her bed when she lived with her host family in New Jersey.

"I was so touched to know the meaning of this pattern. I want to go back to the place I lived with my host family in the 1950s. Now they have passed away. I want to visit there again because I would regain my youth. When I went to America, I was thinking I wanted to be beautiful like before."

Kenny-san." Immediately I recognize Mariko, the interpreter for my interview with Numata-san the last time I was in Hiroshima. She will be my interpreter for today's meeting with Yamaoka Michiko.

Sitting in the living room of the World Friendship Center, I see the streams of multicolored paper cranes that adorn the wall behind Yamaoka-san.

"Since I came back from New York, more than fifty years has already passed," the seventy-five-year-old Yamaoka-san tells me in her deep, considered voice. "In 1955 I desperately wanted to regain my normal appearance. Because America dropped the A-bomb, I thought I deserved medical treatment. Of course I harbored hatred toward not only America but also the Japanese government. That's because Japan started the war. I met so many good-willed Americans, especially Quakers, so I changed my way of thinking.

Yamaoka-san continues, "Twenty-five girls were chosen as the Hiroshima Maidens. At that time, many people wanted plastic surgery, but they were confused—many behind our back criticized us for going to America, some survivors were maybe jealous because they weren't chosen—because America dropped the A-bomb. They were afraid to get medical treatment in America. Then, soon after our arrival, one of the twenty-five died because of the anesthesia. We were so frightened, but this program started from the grass roots and Reverend Tanimoto. He encouraged us to continue.

"I stayed with a Quaker family in New Jersey and I couldn't speak English. I withdrew myself. I was reluctant to go outside by myself. Twenty-seven times, operations—the total of the medical treatments in Tokyo and in New York. Sometimes they tell me thirty-seven times." Yamaoka-san laughs her gravelly laugh.

"When I was in America, I didn't know how they chose us. I came to know about Norman Cousins and other things. I learned the four criteria for choosing: Keloid burns on face and on arms—clearly I was very disfigured. My father died when I was three, my mother and I lived alone, so we were poor. I was unmarried and young. Also, the possibility of successful medical treatment, which is very American."

"Why do you think that is American?"

"That's why they chose: hint of success of surgery. My neck was attached to my shoulder. Maybe when the doctor saw me in Hiroshima, he thought if skin was grafted I could regain the movement of my neck. Practical. But some people didn't have so many serious keloid scars on their faces. So, I know these were the criteria but I don't know why some people were chosen. One of the Maidens was married but hid this from the press. Only when this Maiden returned to Japan did she have a public wedding ceremony.

"When we returned to Japan in 1956, the Hiroshima Maidens experience stimulated the Japanese government to do something to help the A-bomb survivors in 1957. But after I returned to Japan, I didn't tell my story. Ten years after I returned, my mother became sick and was at the end of life. She told me I should tell my story. After she died, I told my story because my mother saved my life."

Yamaoka-san pauses as if in respect for her mother. When she continues her voice is more emphatic. "For ten years after the A-bomb, I was bullied in Japan because I had a very ugly, grotesque, disfigured face. We didn't have money and a house. My neck was attached to my shoulder, my fingers were attached to each other—I had three fingers attached. I couldn't move my fingers. I was seriously burned; the color of my skin fades day by day. I had keloid scars on my face. I had long hair to hide my face. But I met so many people and they helped me. Friendship and kindness. These meetings changed my way of life. I was fifteen when I was exposed to the A-bomb, so twenty-five when I went to America. I was healed not only physically but emotionally."

"Did people in Japan react differently to you than people in the United States?"

"At the time, we didn't have money, but we were able to use five thousand yen as allowance, all the money we had in America, and of course, we couldn't speak English. The Reverend Tanimoto traveled a lot for fund-raising. You know his appearance for *This Is Your Life*. After the show he raised six thousand dollars."

Yamaoka-san mentions the episode of the popular television show featuring Reverend Tanimoto. The host confronted him not only with old teachers but also with the pilot who dropped the A-bomb. Toward the end of the episode, two Maidens appeared on the show. But their faces were not shown; they were seen in silhouette, like shadow puppets on a screen.

Without prompting, Yamaoka-san, for the first time this afternoon, speaks of her experience when the A-bomb was dropped: How far her house and her workplace were from the hypocenter. The B-29s. Deprivation during the war. The atomic flash.

"I thought I was going to die when the bomb blasted over my head. I was trapped by debris while fires were burning all around me. I was saved by my mother. After the blast, she followed me and didn't give up until she found me. I saw many people die, one after another, and once they drank water, they died soon. The people who jumped into the river died. For a long time, I thought it was a shame to survive when they didn't. So, these hideous things were imprinted in my mind. When I see the river, I remember many corpses are floating."

We are silent.

"During the war I worked as a mobilized student. Before that I worked at an ammunition factory to make parachutes. So, for ten years after the war, I didn't go out but worked to make some dresses at home. After I came back from America, I started to make dresses again at home. Some parachutes use silk. I didn't know when I worked in the factory that the material was silk. I changed that parachute into a dress."

"How do you feel being called a Hiroshima Maiden?"

"At first I felt Hiroshima Maidens means unmarried, but there are some married women, so I thought it was strange. But now there is no problem to be called Hiroshima Maidens. That is a true fact. I went to America. At that time, I desperately wanted to regain my normal appearance. That is the only reason I went to America."

"When you came back to Japan, did people react to you differently because you looked different?"

Yamaoka-san immediately understands my question and doesn't wait for the translation. "After I came back—"

"She understands your English," Mariko says. We all laugh.

"People said, oh, you look beautiful, but before that they bullied me using some words, saying cruel things to me. After that they didn't say."

"Did you need more plastic surgery?"

"I received no more plastic surgery. But I had cancer. When my mother passed away, I lost hope to live, so I attempted to commit suicide.

"At that time Pope John Paul visited Hiroshima, and I was hospitalized because of breast cancer. I lost my mother. I was in despair and I had no hope. The pope had a parade. I could see the parade of the pope from the window of Dr. Hanada's hospital. From the window, I looked down at the parade and the pope looked up. Maybe I wore the whitest gown and made it very visible from the window, so I waved at him and the pope looked at me, the pope waved me back. So, I decided not to kill myself. Later, I started to work at the kindergarten."

The interview comes to an end. "That was wonderful," Mariko tells me. "I've been interpreting for Yamaoka-san for years and I never heard her be so open as she is with you."

I wonder what it was that allowed Yamaoka-san to be so open with me. Was it my disability? Did she sense that I, like her, was battling something inside my body that I could not control?

"Where can I get some of these wonderfully colored paper cranes?" I ask the American couple who runs the center.

"Take these with you." A Japanese staff member takes three streams of paper cranes—pink, red, turquoise, green, yellow, purple, and white—off the wall. When she hands them to me, I am glad to have them. But how will I take them back to Tokyo? Where in my tiny room will I put them?

Back at the hotel, I look at the colorful paper cranes, which I've draped over the room's utilitarian desk chair. I notice the blue and yellow cranes match the color of my pills. I think of how Yamaoka-san, wanting to regain her normal appearance, learned to transform a parachute into a dress when she realized they were both made of silk.

And like the first time I was in Hiroshima, it is not the numbers or the facts I most remember. What remains with me is the primordial struggle to survive. After experiencing unimaginable horrors, with a future sure to be filled with a barrage of physical and emotional trauma, by both chance and force of will Yamaoka-san is here to tell me her story.

I think of how Nagasaki was not the original target of the second A-bomb; the original target was Kokura. Both Nagasaki and Kokura were overcast on the morning of August 9, 1945. Nagasaki's Mitsubishi Steel Works became the target only because an opening in the clouds appeared.

I don't know why some people were chosen.

I think of those who did not survive, or did not get treatment, and it is as if I am once again in the cemetery on Kōyasan, in front of the *jizu* statues before crossing over the river to Kobō Daishi's grave. I am once again confronting my dead.

I think of how many have been lost to a virus, including my ex-boyfriend Alex. During a time when there were no medications to stop the progression of the virus and the damage it wrought, he followed every possible lead for some semblance of cure. When hope came in the form of medication, he died not of a virus-related illness but from a heart attack caused by side effects of the still-untested drug that could have—might have—saved his life. Alex, like so many others then and now, like those who lived in Hiroshima and Nagasaki, was in the wrong place at the wrong time.

I know the dangers of one specific horror are not comparable to another. But I also know that what Yamaoka-san told me contains something that is now becoming very familiar to me. Is Yamaoka-san's wave from the visiting pope any different from my drinking from the healing waters of Kiyomizu-dera's spring?

Even in a world where one person's water leads to death, while another's might lead to some kind of healing, some of us—those who survive—cling to whatever hope we may find.

The next day I need a break. I take the train into the mountains to Tsuwano, the small town where in 1867 a group of twenty-eight Christian men were exiled.

In Tsuwano's Tonomachi district of well-preserved old samurai houses of cross-hatched black-and-white plaster walls, the streets are bordered by narrow canals filled with carp. The carp outnumber the town's residents more than ten to one. The fish were originally bred as emergency food in the event of famine.

The Christian exiles were imprisoned in an old, abandoned temple. When the twenty-eight men refused to denounce their religion, they were caged and put outside in the harsh cold winter.

Soon, they were joined by 125 of the Urakami Christians. Before the persecution ended, 36 had died as martyrs, 54 had outwardly apostatized, and 63 remained faithful Christians.

It starts to snow.

On the main street, behind white tile-capped walls is the Catholic Church. Is deep religious belief a form of hope?

I go into the church and am surprised by the combination of stained-glass windows and tatami floors.

The next morning I leave Hiroshima. I carry the unruly strand of multi-colored paper cranes over my shoulder as if it were a suit I will need during my travels.

As the *shinkansen* rushes me back to Tokyo, I feel as if, having put aside thoughts of death for so many years, these thoughts—if not death itself—are catching up to me. Disabled at birth, throughout my life I always wondered how long, and in what situations, I would remain mobile. Then, last summer I began to wonder when the blood clots might return.

And a month later, the knowledge of the virus exacerbated this uncertainty. Staying healthy, and the constant vigilance this required, began to predominate. Now, when I take my attention off the present, even if I propel my thoughts into the future, with increasing clarity, I see death. Since being hospitalized last August, these thoughts at first startled me. But now they're always present. Even when kept at bay for extended periods of time, which is difficult and enervating to do, these thoughts have become more familiar—too familiar.

Over time, will these thoughts of death—if not death itself—enter my life more like the Japanese enter a room, with a slightly embarrassed "*shitsurei shimasu*"? Or will they enter more triumphantly, successfully squeezing out the rest of my life?

My first time in Japan, I arrived alone, anxiously wondering how the Japanese would react to my disability. Soon after arriving, I realized that what I felt about being disabled had been internalized from what I learned from the society in which I lived. In Japan, treated more as a *gaijin* than a person with a disability, I learned to see my different body as nothing more, or less, than a physical fact.

But since that day in Dr. Shay's office almost six months ago, a new layer has been added to my life. For the first time, I felt as if, physically, there was a *before* and an *after*.

I think about Sato-san and Yamaoka-san, how they both wanted to look "normal" and "beautiful" again. I wonder if they are familiar with Tanizaki's Shunkin, who didn't want to be seen once her face was scarred.

If my time with Yamaoka-san illuminated the desperate struggle going on within me and my need to retain, even create, hope, my time with Sato-san brought to the surface and reinforced my feeling of wanting to go back to *before*, a time of less knowledge, of more innocence, when I wasn't aware of what was going on inside my body.

I wanted to be beautiful like before.

I want Sato-san and Yamaoka-san to feel they are as beautiful as they were before the bomb was dropped, before their surgery, as beautiful as I found them as they talked to me.

Born disabled, I never had a "before" before. Nor did I ever have a place in which I wasn't, in some way, different. But now it feels as if I have lost something. Is it loss that I'm feeling? Is *loss* the right word?

The image of the butoh dancer Waguri Yukio digging up a body reappears. As John Lennon sings "Love Is Real," the black curtain parts, revealing the shrine lit by Christmas lights. Will the dancer rebury the body he holds in his arms? Or will he continue to dance with the body that could be his own?

In Japan I wanted to understand the big picture of how those who are physically different are viewed in a culture other than my own. Intentions shift; weather changes. Now, I am on the verge of a visceral understanding that the body, disabled or otherwise, is a fact of a mortal life, a continuum with no before, no after.

Mono no aware. My understanding of disability and Japan merges: All bodies, at one time or another, for one reason or another, or no apparent reason at all, mutate, alter. The body, like Japan, is a process, not fixed in appearance, ability, or time.

Back home, I drape the multicolored paper cranes over the corner chair by the table and the window, the only place in my tiny room to put them in my line of sight.

Eight

Positive Effects

What is love without plans? Without a future?

Years ago, I wrote these words soon after I found out Alex was positive. Then, I was negative. Our relationship did not survive for reasons beyond the virus.

Now it is April. It is still winter in Sapporo. The sidewalks around Mike's apartment are still packed with snow. His apartment is as cold as it was in February.

Together again, we slowly absorb new information. We begin to ask questions, first silently, then with each other. What might the changes in our lives mean?

Our plan to remain together in Japan must be scrapped. Mike will not renew his teaching contract. At the end of August, he will return to Canada. Because of the difficulties of getting the drugs and consistent medical attention I might need, living here seems impossible. I, too, once again, will reluctantly leave Japan.

But I know the vagaries of long-distance relationships. I do not want to live apart from Mike.

In bed, I ask, tentatively, "After my Fulbright ends, do you want me to extend my stay and live here with you in Sapporo this summer?"

"Yes."

In the shower, more boldly, I ask, "Do you want us to figure out a way I can live with you in Canada?"

He doesn't respond.

Our shower complete, drying me with a towel, he finally replies, "Nothing would make me happier."

These desires spoken, we work our way forward to the end of June, when my Fulbright ends.

If well enough, I will travel to Tōno, where many Japanese folktales originated, to complete my research on disability in Japanese culture.

I will mail order a summer's worth of medication, which Reiko will send to Japan. Then, I will join Mike in Sapporo at the end of June.

We will spend the summer together in Sapporo, and Mike will fly with me back to North America. I will show him my place in Northampton. We will go to New York City, another place Mike has never been, where I will introduce him to my friends, to Ian, and to my parents.

"Sounds good," he says.

"I just hope my body cooperates."

"Have you taken your pills?" he asks before we go to bed.

Back in Tokyo, I go to draw blood for another T-cell count as well as to find out the viral load. Returning from the lab, I am surprised to see a cherry tree in early blossom. The first sakura I see in Japan are right on the street where I live.

Not feeling well, I stay in my room for a few days before venturing out again. Most of the time, I don't know if what I am feeling are emotions or physical symptoms. Which is which? Or is the separation arbitrary?

At night, to minimize the side effects, I have to make sure I eat dinner early, preferably around six o'clock and never after eight. If I go out, I have to return early. Twenty minutes after I take my pills, which I'm scheduled to do at eleven, the side effects take hold. After that I'm not steady enough to be outside. I get up late because if I get up earlier in the morning, I'm too dizzy, too nauseous.

What finally propels me outside is my wanting to see the sakura. I have read they have begun to blossom all over Tokyo. The Japanese are mad for flowers, and this madness increases exponentially for cherry blossoms. Perhaps Shōnagon Sei says it best: *After all, do people tire of cherry trees because they blossom every spring?*

Two subway stops from where I live is the Meguro-gawa, listed as one of the top ten places to view cherry blossoms in Tokyo. After the short walk from the station, I see the flags and lanterns hung for the area's sakura festival.

When I turn the corner: countless cherry trees filled with billowy white blossoms, with a hint of pink, hanging over the river. I have never seen such an abundance of flowers. They remind me of the *ukiyo-e* woodblock prints that were the first images I had of Japan.

I think of all the stories I've heard and collected since first arriving in Japan. Who knows which of these stories is fact, which is legend?

The sun starts to set. The shallow water reflects the white blossoms as well as the dark trees. The lanterns are lit; they too are reflected. As I walk on the side of the river, I notice more and more blossoms floating in the water.

To the Japanese, I know that sakura speak to the ephemeral, to mortality, to change.

But, as I felt when I first saw the plum blossoms last month, at the moment I look at the blossoms, there is only the sensation of being sated, filled, by looking at what is in front of me.

Though I am standing still, it feels as if I am moving. Am I still dizzy? Or is my body reacting to what I am seeing?

Even though I will have the opportunity to see more sakura, I know I will never forget this first viewing of the cherry blossoms. That I was able to see what I saw today gives me hope, which I wish will not be as fleeting as the blossoms.

As I watch the cherry blossoms, each one seemingly alone, floating on the shallow river, I remember the plum blossoms so colorful on the ground.

The phone rings, and I don't know where I am. I must have fallen asleep on the floor. I have no idea how I've gotten tangled up in the colored paper cranes, which are usually on the chair on the other side of the room.

The doctor tells me my T cells are back to 344, roughly where they were when I first found out the news before departing for Japan.

Surprisingly, now the virus can no longer be detected in my blood. Even though the test only measures what can be found in blood, and the virus is known to reside in organ tissues and in the brain, this is good news. Usually, after starting the meds, getting to the undetectable level can take many months.

Once again I go with Mika to Mogi-sensei, the healer, to see if he can be of any help with the still-present side effects. Did his last treatment help decrease the amount of virus in my body? Will he notice the change?

After the initial lifting of my right arm and pressing on my shoulder, after prying apart my thumb from my forefinger, after holding onto the moving table and having an acupuncture needle placed briefly in my head, Mogi-sensei looks at me once again from across the room.

"The virus is gone from your lungs and where I saw it last time. It now is only in your brain."

On the train back to Tokyo, I ask Mika if she had mentioned the most recent test results to Mogi-sensei.

"No, you told me not to tell him. Should I have told him?"

Because of my long history of surgery when I was a child, I have never been comfortable with Western medicine. After I see Mogi-sensei, the effects on my day-to-day life are noticeable: more energy, more focus. I probably will never understand what Mogi-sensei does, but the positive effects of his treatments will keep me going to him whenever I can.

Nine

|||||||

New Stories
in an Ancient Land

Oguri Hangan was the son of a fifteenth-century provincial lord who lost his estate to a rival clan. He was known for his horsemanship. His legend, told in Bunraku, Kabuki, and Sekkyu narrative singing, stemmed from his adventures to find his father's stolen heirlooms.

In the legend, Oguri Hangan wanders throughout Japan. In one of the eastern provinces, he reaches the estate of Daizen. Terute, Daizen's daughter, falls in love with him. Daizen tries to kill him first with a wild horse and then by poison. His face scarred, his legs weak (symptoms usually associated with leprosy), Oguri Hangan roams around Japan on a cart, depending on others who faithfully believe that pulling his cart will bring them great merit.

Finally, reaching a waterfall in the sacred land of Kurano, Oguri Hangan is healed by a local hermit and the Yunomine spring's healing waters.

There is still one remaining thing I need to research for the Fulbright Commission presentation. Tōno, home to the folktales known as the *Tōno monogatari*, is remote, far from Tokyo. I wish Mike could accompany me as we originally planned. To make the trip easier, I will make some stops on my way to and from Tōno.

After taking enough pills plus a week's supply in case I'm delayed, I go north, like the poet Bashō did in 1699.

Ever since first arriving in Japan, I've wanted to see the places Bashō saw and wrote about in *Narrow Road to the Interior*.

Now, I stand on the same shore where Bashō once stood. He also looked at the hundreds of small islands and their sharp-angled twisted pines. Using only the name of the place—*Matsu* = pine, *shima* = island— and *ya*, a syllable of both subject and exclamation, Bashō wrote one of his most famous *haiku*:

> *Matsushima ya*
> *ah Matsushima ya*
> *Matsushima ya*

I take a boat to get closer to the small pine islands. I remember my Sensō-ji fortune of almost eight months ago and think of Mike: *Polling a boat across the stream is a simile of your getting along well with others in this world.*

Hiraizumi was once the resplendent capital of the Fujiwara clan, who chose it to be their paradise on earth. Now, Hiraizumi is a sleepy town

on the banks of the Kitakami-gawa. I've come here to see the garden at
Mōtsū-ji, the ancient site of *waka* parties, an inspiration for my first
poems about Japan.

I arrive in the early evening and check in at the Mōtsū-ji *shukubo*.
Tonight I'm the only guest at the temple hostel.

Despite the early morning side effects of the drugs, I'm up at dawn
so I can join the monks in the main hall for prayers. The young monk
who checked me into my room is the only monk present. I sit across
from him. I am still a bit dizzy. As he chants this morning's sutra, I close
my eyes. Once again, I remember my Sensō-ji fortune—*your wish will
come true, so you should be modest for everything*. I ask my body to get me
safely where I want to go.

Mōtsū-ji feels like a ghost temple. After the prayers I walk around
the garden lake. The garden is mostly ruins. I find the remnants of the
stream. Centuries ago this was the focus of the garden's festivities, during
which *waka* parties were held. Here, on the banks of garden's stream,
contestants sat writing short poems before a cup of saké floated by.

I am the only one who gets off the train at Tōno.

In 1909 folklorist Yanagita Kunio visited Tōno. He found a world
populated by demons and spirits that the farmers tried to placate through
ancient rituals. Here, goblins, ghosts, and gods were a part of everyday
life, like Hanada-sensei explained at our meeting three months ago in
Tokyo. It is said that people in Tōno still talk of Zashiki Warashi, a child
spirit who can be heard running at night.

The most popular character of the Tōno legends is the mischievous
kappa.

Walking from the station, I don't notice any goblins or ghosts. But I
do notice the irascible *kappa* all over the town: on postboxes, in souvenir
shops, and even at the *koban*, the police box.

According to legend, the *kappa* lives in the river. Usually, the *kappa* is green, but sometimes he has a red face. He is somewhat frog-like and has long skinny limbs, webbed hands and feet, a sharp beak, and a hollow on the top of his head. This hollow must be kept filled with water. If you meet a *kappa*, it is recommended that you bow. When the *kappa* returns your bow, the water will pour out from the hollow on his head and he will have to hurry off to replenish it.

At the Tōno City Museum, I learn about the belief that women who become pregnant with a *kappa*'s child give birth to deformed babies. When they are born, these babies are hacked to pieces, put into small wine casks, and buried in the ground. I remember the true story of the Yokohama woman who killed her disabled daughter. In Tōno, my research has come full circle.

The next day I take the train and a bus to the middle of nowhere. Here, I am supposed to wait for my next mode of transportation. Mika has made and confirmed my reservation at the 350-year-old Tsurunoyu Onsen, one of the most unspoiled hot springs in all of Japan.

I check my watch: ten minutes to the time when someone from the *onsen* is supposed to pick me up to take me the rest of the way. In no other place but Japan would I be confident that this will happen. Even so, I check my watch a few more times before ten minutes have passed until, as if on cue, a van appears on the otherwise empty road. The van stops. The driver asks, "*Kenny-sama desu ka?*"

"*Hai. Kenny desu.*"

When we turn on to a dirt road and head farther into the mountains, I notice my cell phone has no service. This will be the first night since we met that I will not be able to talk with Mike.

As soon as I'm out of the van, I know I've come to the right place. Beyond a wooden waterwheel and a small rickety *torii*-like gateway is a wide dirt path. On both sides of the path are two-storied wooden buildings. All the wood is rustically painted black. The only sound is of rushing water, which gets louder as I make my way through what seems a cross between a Wild West ghost town and the main street of an Edo-period village. The path ends at the river.

The van driver has followed me. He points across a small bridge that crosses the rushing water. I nod. I know he's pointing to the *rotemburo*, the outdoor hot spring bath, beyond the tall winter-parched reeds that line the other side of the river.

I drop my bags in my small tatami-matted room. I change into a *yukata* and return to the rushing water.

I cross the bridge.

I don't understand the signs. If I understood them, I know they would tell me which changing room and which of the baths is for men. I peer into one of the huts and see a man. I guess this is the one for men. I take off my *yukata* and leave it in a wicker basket.

Outside, I peek around the reed fence and see a man in the pool.

I submerge myself into the close-to-scalding water. I lean back and look up at the surrounding mountains and then the clear sky.

I don't know what is finger or what is toe, what is head or what is sole, what is front or what is behind. Every part of my body individual-ized but coalescing. Skin no barrier. Difference no matter.

I could be a butoh dancer emerging, rising, emerging, ever so slowly; I see life's process not as change but as chang*ing*—

No east. No west. No direction. No plan.

Time dissolves. Thought evaporates.

Conscious, unconscious. Seen, unseen. Everything inside and outside my body merges—

Changing, the virus not me but a part of me.

No words. No feeling. No future.

I disappear.

Epilogue

Procession

When I left Japan the first time, I was supposed to write a report for the foundation that supported my stay. I couldn't. It didn't seem over yet. Now, after presenting my research to the Fulbright Commission, I can write the report.

I don't want to write it. But this time, I know I'll be able to write it because the question I thought I came to answer—what is it like to be disabled in Japan?—has, by living in Japan, been replaced. Through my research, as much as I've been able, what was previously unseen is now seen. I've given at least some visibility to the history of disability in Japan.

And now I finally understand there is no need for a big picture connecting all I have learned. The hedge has been removed: what I see is a continuum of experiences, of stories, and of time. There is no before or after, no arrival or return.

In June, a week before I leave Tokyo, I see the Meiji Jingu irises with Mika.

Even on this overcast day, the irises startle. I walk over the marsh on the wooden bridge. I bend as low as I can to get as close as I can to see each flower.

On the other side of the bridge, I see Mika. She is holding the *tenugui* of my garden poems, which begin with my very first view of the irises, over her head as if it were a banner. I realize it has started to rain.

"You'll still get wet," I tell Mika when I join her.

"It's best to see irises in the rain."

"Who told you that?"

"It's good luck. It's traditional."

We stand watching the raindrops trickle in the marsh of irises.

A week later, I'm getting ready to catch the plane to Sapporo, where I will live with Mike for the summer. All my stuff has either been sent back to the United States or is in the luggage waiting by the door. I scan the room to make sure I haven't left anything behind.

I see the colored stream of paper cranes, still looking like a wig from the 1960s, splayed over my room's only chair like a drunken guest who has stayed too long.

What am I to do with this gift I brought back to Tokyo from Hiroshima?

I could pack it. But the paper would get crumbled. I can't carry them on the plane, like I did on the train, as if they were dry cleaning.

I'm hungry. I want to eat one more time at the noodle shop near the station. I gather the cranes and take them with me.

Halfway down the street, I turn right instead of left. I enter the small local shrine, which I have passed every day I've been able to go outside. I ascend the ten wooden stairs and stand before the familiar wood-slatted offering box. Closing my eyes, I once again pray, bow, and clap.

Instead of throwing coins into the box, I place the cranes in front of the altar. Here, they do not clash with their surroundings as they did in my room. With the fruit, the bottle of saké, and flowers, the cranes comprise a perfect still life of offerings.

I wonder which *kami* might be placated by the offering of this gift that I know, only a short time ago, I would have taken with me, not wanting to let it go.

It is summer in Sapporo. The snow has finally melted.

On the last night of Obon, I go to Nakajima-Kōen, a large park through which flows the Nakajima-gawa. Along the river there is a shrine where the end of Obon is celebrated with a festival whose goal is to assist the ancestral spirits in finding their way home.

Mike will meet me after work. I arrive early with a few other stragglers just before twilight. We watch tables being set up on the side of the rock-lined river. On the river a floating raft-like bridge of wood planks is built.

As the night darkens, the few becomes a crowd. A line forms in front of the table. I join the line.

Each person picks up a bag, a tray, and a candle.

The bags are red or green, each with kanji, reminding me of Chinese take-out food containers. The trays are shallow-lipped, rectangular. The candles are thicker than votive candles but thinner than the *yahrtzeit* memorial candles I remember my father lit in remembrance of his father, my grandfather who died five years before I was born.

I watch what others do and do the same. I put my candle on the tray and cover it with the bag, which I discover has two open ends.

We all look like we're carrying fast food from a park concession. But as each person reaches the makeshift bridge, a black-robed, gray-sashed priest lights each candle, and each of us is transformed.

Candle lit, I bend down and place my tray in the water. I send it off and watch it slowly drift down the river.

One by one, everyone does the same, creating a weaving line of light—green, red, and white—reflecting in the water.

From where I stand, the lights floating down the river look like a fleeing procession of refugees. Some of the floating candle boats bunch up as if in polite, if private, conversation. Others float on, alone.

Occasionally, a group or a single candle get hung up in a patch of reeds or bump against a rock and remain bobbing, not moving forward, on the side of the river. Every now and then, someone braves the steep incline of the shore and gently helps the candle boat on its way.

I don't know which one is my boat, nor do I care. But for some reason, one boat isn't enough. I rejoin the line and, once again, allow my lit candle to join the ever-increasing line floating downstream to where I do not know.

Waiting for Mike, I repeat the candle lighting and send-off countless times. I do not care if the priest thinks I've done this too many times. Even if he does recognize me, he will probably think I'm just another crazy *gaijin*. In the darkness, dressed in his black robe and gray sash, I don't even know if he's the same priest who lit my previous candle.

By the time Mike arrives, the procession has dwindled to a few. He joins me, and together we send off a final candle. We watch the flickering yet steady light drift where the water takes it.

Acknowledgments

In the Province of the Gods could not have been written without the generous support, financial and otherwise, of Creative Capital. Special thanks to Ruby Lerner, Sean Elwood, Lisa Dent, and Kemi Ilesanmi.

I am also grateful for grants from the Toronto Arts Council and Ontario Arts Council; the Japan-U.S. Friendship Commission and the National Endowment for the Arts for the Creative Arts Fellowship to Japan; and the Fulbright Scholar Program for the fellowship supporting the research in Japan for this book.

Thanks to the Leighton Artist Studios at the Banff Centre for the Arts, the Ledig House International Writers Residency, Fondation Ledig-Rowohlt/Château de Lavigny, the MacDowell Colony, and Yaddo for residencies during which much of this book was written; the Canada Council for the Arts for travel funds; the Goddard College Faculty Development Fund for support with research in Matsue; and the Llewellyn Miller Fund, Poets in Need, Edward Albee and the American Academy of Arts and Letters, and Stephen King's Haven Foundation for emergency financial assistance.

Thank you to Mary Johnson and Michael "Roku" Fieni for help in getting to and from Japan.

I am grateful to Christopher Blasdel, Shimumura Naoko, Enbutsu Kimiko, Higuchi Keiko, and the library staff at the International House in Tokyo for assistance in Japan and with research.

Thanks to Nagase Osamu for helping to jumpstart the research in Japan, Kozue Kay Nagata for sending the research gifts in the mail and translating my writing into Japanese, Hanada Shuncho for his disability studies work, Ueno Etsuko at the Japan Society for the Rehabilitation of Disabled Persons for her commitment to those with disabilities in Japan and worldwide, and Matsui Ryosuke for his warmth and guidance as my Fulbright advisor. I am proud to call these Japanese colleagues friends.

Thanks also to Murakami Takako for literary Tokyo, Mochizawa Osamu and family for warm hospitality and the drive to Ando's Museum of Wood, Handa Miho for research assistance and translation of documents, and Dobashi Yoshito for his friendship.

Thank you to Takechi Yuka and Takahashi Kumiko for the collaboration on the songs and Yasuda Yugo for the collaboration on the *tenugui*.

Greg Irwin, Ken Sasaki, Deborah DeSnoo, and Shuji Kikuchi helped make Japan home. Brenda Shaughnessy shared comradeship and butoh exploration.

The World Friendship Center, Nishimoto Masami at the *Chugoku Shimbun*, Miyamoto Keiko, and Yamane Michiko provided assistance in Hiroshima. Numata Suzuko, Sato Michiko, and Yamaoka Michiko trusted me with their stories.

Donald Richie shared his inimitable understanding of Japan and his kindness. I wish you were around to read this book.

Thanks to Andrea Leebron-Clay, Kathryn Levy, David Shohl, Joan Silber, and Chase Twichell for making possible the second stay in Japan and Monica Sharf and Mary Ting for assistance while abroad. I could not have done any of this without your love and support.

I am grateful to Andrea Snyder for artist coaching during the final stages of writing, Elizabeth Wales for her continued belief in my work, and Raphael Kadushin for finding in the book what I knew was there.

Dr. William Shay went beyond a doctor's call and Dr. Randall Marshall gave considerate assistance in navigating the journey.

Joan and Donald Fries, my ever-supportive parents, dealt with yet another difficult situation with aplomb. Without your love, my life could not have happened as it has happened.

The late Matsumoto Masumi gave me a friendship I will always treasure. That you are not here to read this book is a loss beyond words.

Thanks to Mika Kimula, singer, collaborator, friend beyond compare, and in many ways "my Japan."

Rahna Reiko Rizzuto, fellow Japan traveler, provided countless hours of writerly friendship, editorial advice, and an intimate understanding of the foundations of this book. I have always felt this book is as much yours as it is mine.

Ian Jehle, what more can be said: you are still there to share it and form it all with me (and now you too know Japan).

Mike McCulloch, my husband, my lover, my best friend: you are the destination to which this book leads.

Suggested Readings

My work on *In the Province of the Gods* has been greatly assisted by the following books, which I recommend for further reading on subjects and themes written about in the book.

In the Gardens of Japan, the poems I wrote in Japan that are mentioned in the book, will be published by Garden Oak Press in conjunction with the publication of *In the Province of the Gods*.

Bashō. *The Narrow Road to the Interior: And Other Writings*. Translated by Sam Hamill. Boston: Shambhala Classics, 2000.

Hearn, Lafcadio. *Glimpses of Unfamiliar Japan*. Various editions.

———. *Kwaidan: Stories and Studies of Strange Things*. Various editions.

———. *Lafcadio Hearn's Japan: An Anthology of His Writings on the Country and Its People*. Edited by Donald Richie. New York: Tuttle, 2011.

Keane, Marc Peter. *The Art of Setting Stones: And Other Writings from the Japanese Garden*. Berkeley: Stone Bridge Press, 2002.

Morris, Ivan. *The Pillow Book of Sei Shōnagon*. New York: Columbia University Press, 1967.

Richie, Donald. *The Inland Sea*. Berkeley: Stone Bridge Press, 2015.

———. *The Japan Journals: 1947–2004*. Edited by Leza Lowitz. Berkeley: Stone Bridge Press, 2005.

———. *A Lateral View: Essays on Culture and Style in Contemporary Japan*. Berkeley: Stone Bridge Press, 1992.

Saikuku Iharu. *The Great Mirror of Male Love*. Translated by Paul Gordon Schalow. Stanford: Stanford University Press, 2003.

Tschumi, Christian. *Mirei Shigemori: Modernizing the Japanese Garden*. Berkeley: Stone Bridge Press, 2007.

Kenny Fries is the author of *Body, Remember: A Memoir* and *The History of My Shoes and the Evolution of Darwin's Theory*, winner of the Outstanding Book Award from the Gustavus Myers Center for the Study of Bigotry and Human Rights. He is the editor of *Staring Back: The Disability Experience from the Inside Out* and the author of the libretto for *The Memory Stone*, an opera commissioned by the Houston Grand Opera. His books of poems include *Anesthesia, Desert Walking*, and *In the Gardens of Japan*. He received the Creative Arts Fellowship from the Japan-U.S. Friendship Commission and the National Endowment for the Arts, has twice been a Fulbright Scholar (Japan and Germany), and is the recipient of the prestigious Creative Capital grant, as well as grants from the DAAD (German Academic Exchange), Canada Council for the Arts, Ontario Arts Council, and Toronto Arts Council. He teaches in the MFA in Creative Writing Program at Goddard College.

LIVING OUT

Gay and Lesbian Autobiographies

The Other Mother: A Lesbian's Fight for Her Daughter
Nancy Abrams

An Underground Life: Memoirs of a Gay Jew in Nazi Berlin
Gad Beck

Gay American Autobiography: Writings from Whitman to Sedaris
Edited by David Bergman

Surviving Madness: A Therapist's Own Story
Betty Berzon

You're Not from Around Here, Are You? A Lesbian in Small-Town America
Louise A. Blum

Just Married: Gay Marriage and the Expansion of Human Rights
Kevin Bourassa and Joe Varnell

Two Novels: "Development" and "Two Selves"
Bryher

The Hurry-Up Song: A Memoir of Losing My Brother
Clifford Chase

In My Father's Arms: A Son's Story of Sexual Abuse
Walter A. de Milly III

*Lawfully Wedded Husband: How My Gay Marriage Will Save
    the American Family*
Joel Derfner

Midlife Queer: Autobiography of a Decade, 1971–1981
Martin Duberman

Self-Made Woman: A Memoir
Denise Chanterelle DuBois

The Black Penguin
Andrew Evans

*The Man Who Would Marry Susan Sontag: And Other Intimate Literary
    Portraits of the Bohemian Era*
Edward Field

In the Province of the Gods
Kenny Fries

Body, Remember: A Memoir
Kenny Fries

Travels in a Gay Nation: Portraits of LGBTQ Americans
Philip Gambone

Autobiography of My Hungers
Rigoberto González